בשורת מתי

AN OLD HEBREW TEXT OF
ST. MATTHEW'S GOSPEL

TO

MY WIFE

AND TO MY FELLOW-MEMBERS

OF THE

INTERNATIONAL HEBREW CHRISTIAN ALLIANCE

THIS BOOK IS AFFECTIONATELY

DEDICATED

בשורת מתי

AN OLD HEBREW TEXT OF
ST. MATTHEW'S GOSPEL

TRANSLATED, WITH AN INTRODUCTION
NOTES AND APPENDICES

BY

HUGH J. SCHONFIELD

38 George Street T. & T. CLARK Edinburgh
1927

PRINTED IN GREAT BRITAIN BY
MORRISON AND GIBB LIMITED

FOR

T. & T. CLARK, EDINBURGH

LONDON: SIMPKIN, MARSHALL, HAMILTON, KENT, AND CO. LIMITED
NEW YORK: CHARLES SCRIBNER'S SONS

PREFACE

EVERY effort that can be put forth to illuminate the pages of Holy Writ should commend itself to those who have made its teaching their rule of life, and such an effort has been humbly attempted in the present volume. The Bible has suffered greatly at the hands of faulty expositors who, from ignorance of the languages in which it is written, have based their interpretations on forms of words found in a translation. The Bible has suffered equally at the hands of inaccurate translators. A literal translation is not necessarily a good one. The translator may be out of sympathy with his author, or he may be insufficiently acquainted with the customs, modes of thought, and colloquial expressions of the author's people. The more remote the date of the document, the more difficult becomes the task of understanding precisely the meaning of the terms employed. It is not by any means an exaggerated statement to assert that at the present day it is still impossible to make a correct translation of the whole Bible. None the less, we have advanced far beyond the meagre information possessed by those who prepared the Authorised Version. And almost every year throws fresh light on the social, religious and philological conditions of which the Bible is the mouthpiece.

The work of the translator is thus seen to be beset with difficulties even when he has the original in his hands, but in the case of the Bible he has to face further complications. Not only are the originals lost, but accurate copies are also unobtainable. This necessitates the preparation of a critical edition, based on the divergent texts of manuscripts of varying age and authenticity, before the translation can be begun ; and even so, such a critical text is liable at any time to be invalidated by the discovery of older and more faithful copies of the original documents. There is still another eventuality to be taken into consideration : the supposed originals of certain books of the Bible may themselves be translations. This would be analogous to our expecting that a French version of Shakespeare made from a German translation of that poet's works would accurately represent the sense of the original English text. Broadly speaking, we take Hebrew as being the language in which the writings of the Old Testament were composed, and Greek for the New ; but this cannot be asserted dogmatically. Apart from the fact that, in the Old Testament as we have it, there are certain sections of the Books of Daniel and Ezra written not in Hebrew but in Aramaic, we can by no means be sure that some of the earlier narratives of the Bible were not written in ancient Babylonian or Egyptian. When we turn to the New Testament we find that there are reasons for suspecting a Hebrew or Aramaic original for the Gospels of Matthew, Mark and John, and for the Apocalypse.

In the case of Matthew's Gospel, with which this volume is immediately concerned, the evidence is particularly strong, for we have the categorical statement of primitive Christian tradition to this effect. Whether the Hebrew, or Aramaic, Matthew referred to by tradition be the same as that which now goes by his name in our Bible cannot be discussed here. My own opinion is that the canonical Gospel is an abridged edition of a larger work, of which fragments still survive, and which contained all and more of the acts and sayings of Christ than is now found in the four accepted Gospels put together. I believe that this Protevangel was written in Hebrew, not in Aramaic, and was intended by the Judæan Christians who produced it to become the last book of the Old Testament canon, such a collection as the New Testament not having at that time been thought of. Whatever may have been its original title, we have early allusions to it under the name of " the Gospel," " the Gospel of the Lord," " the Gospel of the Twelve, or, of the Apostles," " the Gospel of the Hebrews " and " the Hebrew Matthew." As to this document being intended to complete the canon of the Old Testament, I might quote in support of this suggestion the statement of the Judæo-Christian historian, Hegesippus, in the second century that " in every city, that prevails which the Law, and the Prophets, and the Lord enjoin."

If the canonical Gospel of Matthew has been translated from a Hebrew or Aramaic original, or, as I have suggested, is an abridged edition in Greek from a larger Hebrew work, we should expect to find some evidences of the translator's hand. Such evidences manifest themselves in different ways, but commonly in misreadings of the original text. Good results have already been obtained in the case of certain obscure passages in some of the Jewish apocalyptic writings, preserved in Greek, whose Hebrew or Aramaic origin was suspected, by retranslation into these languages. This has often not only revealed the source of error, but at the same time confirmed the theory of translation. The early Hebrew MS. of the Gospel of Matthew translated in the present work enables us to apply this test more or less effectively to the Greek text of this Gospel, and the results obtained prove to my mind conclusively the existence of an underlying Hebrew original.

In the introductory chapters I have traced the history of the Hebrew manuscript as far as it was possible to do so, and have given my reasons for supposing the Greek text to be a translation. If I am correct, the Hebrew Gospel must necessarily represent something of the original force of the diction, and even in its English dress should afford the reader a deeper insight into the true significance of the utterances of the Christ, and the incidents of His life.

HUGH J. SCHONFIELD.

CONTENTS

PART I

INTRODUCTION

CHAPTER I

DESCRIPTION AND HISTORY OF THE MS.

In the spring of 1925 the writer purchased from a London antiquarian bookseller a small volume, dated A.D. 1555, containing the Gospel of Matthew in Hebrew, followed by a series of Jewish objections to the Gospel to the number of twenty-three, also in Hebrew. The text of the Gospel was accompanied at the end of the volume by a Latin translation. A dedicatory epistle to Charles de Guise, Cardinal of Lorraine, relates how Jean du Tillet, Bishop of Brieu, while travelling in Italy in the year 1553, found the Hebrew manuscript among the Jews, and brought it back with him to Paris, where he commissioned a Hebrew scholar, Jean Mercier, to translate it into Latin. Mercier, however, has a slightly different tale to tell. In his own preface he states that the Bishop of Brieu had extorted the MS. from the Jews of Rome for the purpose of examination. Confirmatory evidence of this statement appears in the

fact that, on 12th August 1553, Pope
Julius III. signed a decree for the sup-
pression of the Talmud on the representation of the anti-Semitic Pietro, Cardinal
Caraffa, the Inquisitor-General, afterwards
Pope Paul IV. This decree was carried
into effect in Rome with great ruthless-
ness on Rosh Hashanna (Jewish New Year's
Day), 9th September 1553, for not only
were copies of the Talmud seized, on the
plea that it was inimical to Christianity,
but every Hebrew book on which the
minions of the Inquisition could lay their
hands. It is highly probable that the
Bishop of Brieu found the Hebrew MS. of
Matthew's Gospel among the confiscated
books.

Such a Gospel of ancient date written
in the sacred tongue was sufficient to awaken
in the mind of a student of New Testament
literature the liveliest curiosity, especially
in view of the settled tradition of the Church
that the Gospel of Matthew was the only
New Testament document that could lay
definite claim to a Hebrew original. This
curiosity was considerably increased when
the writer discovered that the Hebrew MS.
differed in a number of places from the
Received Text. It was felt that the subject

would well repay further investigation, and
information was sought for which might
throw light on its antecedents. No ascription of authorship apparently attached
to the MS., and both du Tillet and his
collaborator, Mercier, seemed uncertain
what to make of it. Practically all the
available information on the subject which
the writer has been able to obtain will be
found in the following pages, together with
such inferences as it was possible to draw
from a study of the text itself.

Two title-pages accompany the 1555
edition, one at each end of the volume.
The former reads as follows : " The Gospel
of Matthew faithfully rendered out of the
Hebrew (Evangelium Matthaei ex Hebraeo
fideliter redditum) " ; while at the foot of
the page, also in Latin, is the name of the
publisher, Martin Le Jeune, and the date,
Paris, 1555. The latter title-page is in
Hebrew and Latin, and describes the volume
as " The Gospel of Matthew, until this day
laid up among the Jews and concealed in
their recesses, and now at last, from out of
their apartments and from darkness, brought
forth into the light, etc."

בשורת מתי עד היום הזה כמוסה עם היהודים
ונחבאה במערותם ועתה באחרונה מתוך הדריהם

ומחושך מוצאת לאור שנת הנ"ך הרה ויולדת
בן לפ"ק מגאולתנו פה בפאריס האם בצרפת:

The Latin subscription adds the further
information that the text of the Vulgate
has been followed wherever possible in
translating the Hebrew Gospel into the
Latin tongue (Evangelium Hebraicum
Matthaei, recens e Iudaeorum penetralibus
erutum, cum interpretatione Latina, ad
vulgatam quoad fieri potuit, accommodata).

Besides the copy in the writer's posses-
sion, other copies of the 1555 edition are
in the following British libraries : the
British Museum, the Bodleian Library at
Oxford and the Library of the British and
Foreign Bible Society in London.

The original MS. from which du Tillet's
edition was taken is now in the Bibliothèque
Nationale at Paris, and is catalogued under
Hebrew MSS., No. 132.

No new edition of the text appeared, so
far as the writer is aware, until 1879, when
it was re-edited with an introduction and
notes by Dr. Adolf Herbst, under the title
of " Des Schemtob ben Schaphrut hebraeische
Übersetzung des Evangeliums Matthaei, nach
den Drucken des S. Münster und J. du
Tillet-Mercier " (Göttingen, 1879).

This title requires explanation. Dr.

Herbst believed that the du Tillet MS. and another Hebrew version of Matthew's Gospel, published by Sebastian Münster in 1537, were both dependent on the Hebrew translation of this Gospel, believed to have been made by a Jewish writer named Shem-Tob ben Shaprut, and found in his *Touchstone*, A.D. 1385.

Dr. Herbst contented himself in his introduction, which is frequently quoted in this chapter, with enumerating the notices made by earlier scholars of Münster's and du Tillet's editions, and reached his conclusions largely on their testimony. By his own admission, he had not gone very deeply into the problem, and it has therefore been left to the present writer to deal more fully with the whole subject, and to present the first translation of du Tillet's Gospel into any modern language.

As the crux of the whole problem is the relationship which the versions of Shem-Tob, Münster and du Tillet bear to one another, we will make this our first concern.

Shem-Tob ben Shaprut was a famous Jewish polemical writer, and flourished in the fourteenth century in Spain. His chief controversial work אבן בוחן, *The Touchstone*, has never been printed, and is only found in manuscript. A copy is in the British Museum, Oriental Department, Add. No. 26964. It is divided into fifteen sections, of which the twelfth contains the Hebrew version of Matthew. The text of the Gospel is divided into ninety-seven chapters. After the first and most of the others follow notes and queries headed, "Shem Tob the ancient saith," or, "The ancient saith." It is full of lacunæ, and though often agreeing with du Tillet's text, presents very considerable differences. In the first chapter alone the following variations from du Tillet occur. Shem-Tob's text speaks of Rachab as "the harlot," it omits the names of Jotham and Ahaz; further on omits the names of Eliakim, Azzur and Zadok, and finally renders Matt. 1 : 16 as, "Jacob begat Joseph ; he, Joseph, was the husband of Miriam (there is a lacuna here) who is called Messiah, in the foreign tongue, Kristos." The last clause in particular is more like a paraphrase than a translation.

There is even room for doubt as to whether Shem-Tob was himself the author of the translation contained in *The Touchstone*. In the previous century, Raymund Martini, a Spanish Dominican, in a controversial work,

entitled *Pugio Fidei* (The Poignard of Faith),
made use of a Hebrew translation of
Matthew which is more like Shem-Tob's
than du Tillet's, and was in existence before he was born. Martini only quotes
from the second chapter of Matthew, but
both Shem-Tob and he agree in calling
the Wise Men, Astrologers, while the
du Tillet version accurately calls them
Magicians.

The principal witness brought forward by
Dr. Herbst to prove the identity of du Tillet's
text with that of Shem-Tob is a Hebrew
Christian, by name Johannes-Baptista Jonas,
who published a Hebrew translation of the
four Gospels at Rome, A.D. 1668. Jonas
seems to have had a similar experience to
that of the writer. In his Hebrew introduction he says : " I found in a bookseller's a
certain book purporting to be the Gospel of
Matthew until this day hidden on the part
of the Jews, and concealed in their recesses,
but now at last brought forth into the light,
etc. And when I saw it, I rejoiced more
than at any fortune. But when I read it
I was in doubt as to whether he who copied
it out was inexpert in the sacred language,
or that the Jews copied it out in faulty
language in order to discredit it in the eyes

of the reader, so that he might not give it consideration. While in this quandary, lo, God brought to my notice a certain book, whose title was *The Touchstone*, by a Jew named Shem-Tob Shaprut, who had copied out in the same faulty language the Gospel of Matthew, and after each section an objection against the Gospel, and likewise in the book chanced upon in Paris, at the end are twenty-eight (*sic*) objections which the Jews objected against the Gospel, etc."

On the above testimony Dr. Herbst remarks : " It follows from this, therefore, as a definite conclusion that the author of the translation of the Gospel of Matthew published by du Tillet is Shem-Tob Shaprut " (Herbst, pp. 8, 9).

With all due consideration to Dr. Herbst, the writer fails to see how the statement of Jonas warrants so positive a conclusion. Jonas certainly says that both versions were written in similar language, but that does not prove verbal identity, which we have seen not to have been the case. Such language was common enough in early Rabbinical literature. Further, many of the important variant readings found in du Tillet's text are entirely absent from

Shem-Tob's. Neither can the fact that both versions are accompanied by objections against the Gospel be shown to prove anything. In *The Touchstone* the objections are made by the author in his own name, and follow the chapters of the text, while in the du Tillet MS. they are grouped at the end, and no authorship is ascribed to them. They are not even identical, and Shem-Tob has many more than du Tillet.

The utmost that can be inferred from a comparison of the two versions is that they may both depend on an older Hebrew translation, which may equally be said of Martini's text. As far back as the fourth century we hear of a Hebrew Matthew preserved in the Jewish archives at Tiberias (see Appendix A).

Münster's version, on the other hand, seems to be half-way between Shem-Tob and du Tillet. This version was published under the title of תורת המשיח (The Law of Messiah), "Evangelium secundum Matthaeum in Lingua Hebraica, cum versione Latina atque succinctis annotationibus" (Basiliæ, 1537). Münster states in his dedication to Henry VIII. that he received the Hebrew translation from the Jews in a defective condition, and with many lacunæ, which he took upon himself to fill in (" Matthaei evangelium in nativa sua, hoc est Hebraica lingua, non qualiter apud Hebraeorum vulgus lacerum inveni, sed a me redintegratum et in unum corpus redactum emittemus ") (Herbst, p. 1).

The fact that Münster's text is so largely his own work renders it valueless for all critical purposes. Du Tillet, in his dedicatory epistle, comparing the MS. discovered by him with this version, says : " It differs equally from the sort of thing, usually awkward and inappropriate, which Münster foists upon us." With this estimate we are in full agreement. Münster draws attention to the defective state in which he received the Hebrew Gospel; and the lacunæ which so frequently occur in his text and that of Shem-Tob, from which du Tillet's MS. is practically free, provides an additional argument against identification.

The authorship of the Hebrew Matthew must therefore be left an open question, though there is a strong probability that it did not originate with Shem-Tob Shaprut, but dates from an earlier period. The relationship of the various MSS. may reasonably be shown thus :

UNKNOWN HEBREW VERSION OF MATTHEW'S GOSPEL.

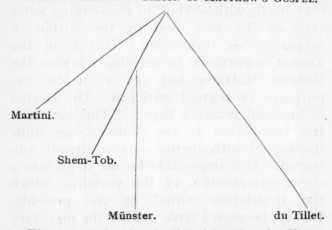

Martini.

Shem-Tob.

Münster.   du Tillet.

There can be no doubt that the du Tillet MS. remains in undisputed possession of the field as the oldest and most complete Hebrew version of any part of the New Testament at present known. It has, therefore, a peculiar interest in many ways. Firstly, because it reveals the interest taken by Jews in the person of Christ from an early date, and, secondly, because it was just this Gospel, of Matthew, which was believed by the Church to have been originally written in Hebrew, and which in various recensions persisted for centuries among the Judæo-Christian communities of Palestine and Syria.

We turn now to a consideration of the text itself, with a view to discovering what type of MS. was used by the author in preparing his translation. This is of the utmost importance in deciding whether the Hebrew Matthew has any value for the purposes of textual criticism. Dr. Herbst in his final remarks says : " The source of the translation is the Vulgate, as some theological introductions have already observed. It is impossible for me to go into a closer examination of the variants, which the translation edited by me presents. Firstly, because I have neither the necessary materials nor the time and opportunity for looking them up and utilising them, and, further, because an exhaustive treatise on the subject would be too voluminous " (Herbst, p. 16).

If the source of the translation is the Vulgate, there is an end to the matter ; but an examination of the variant readings, neglected by Dr. Herbst, clearly shows that, though the text as a whole may be said to be more closely allied to the Vulgate than to any other known MS. or version, there are sufficient striking differences to render it at least doubtful if this was the source. By appending to his introduction lists in

which he first of all gives the places where
the Hebrew supports the Received Greek
Text against the Vulgate, then the places
where the reverse is the case, and finally
the passages in which the Hebrew differs
from both, Dr. Herbst clearly acknowledges
that his assertion is not borne out by the
facts.

Had Dr. Herbst had the time to pursue
his investigations further, he would have
been surprised to find that certain of the
readings which he catalogues are attested by
other ancient authorities such as the Old
Latin and Old Syriac versions, and even
the apocryphal *Book of James*, which would
hardly have been the case if the Vulgate
had been the source of the translation.
There is always the possibility, of course,
that the translator used more than one
text in preparing his Hebrew Gospel, but
this is not likely.

Again, the du Tillet text possesses char-
acteristic features in common with the lost
Aramaic Gospel of Matthew, commonly
known as *The Gospel of the Hebrews*.   These
are described by E. B. Nicholson as—(1)
close affinity with Matthew ; (2) less close,
but still marked affinity with Luke ; (3)
decided independence of both.   (*The Gospel*

according to the Hebrews, London, 1879, p. 143).

Another point of agreement between the Gospel of the Hebrews and the du Tillet MS. is their use of the Hebrew in preference to the Septuagint for all the Old Testament quotations. This last statement respecting the form of quotation in the Aramaic Matthew is made on the authority of Jerome, who translated it into Greek and Latin (see Appendix B). It is to Jerome that the revision of the Latin version, known as the Vulgate, is due, and it is not impossible that he may have incorporated into his revised text readings from the Aramaic Gospel which he held in high esteem. The agreements between the Vulgate and the du Tillet MS. might then be attributed to the ultimate dependence of both on the earlier Aramaic Matthew.

In many instances the readings of the Hebrew are a distinct improvement on the Received Text ; in some cases even restoring obvious omissions : the reader is referred to the next chapter for a discussion on the more interesting of these. The internal evidence seems to point to an unknown text of slightly " Western " tendencies, and of uncertain date and language, as the source of the Hebrew Matthew.

In summarising the results, the present writer is not satisfied that in the du Tillet MS. of Matthew's Gospel we have merely a Hebrew version of the Vulgate made by a mediæval translator. There are many early traditional elements in the text which cannot be accounted for in this way. In the following chapter, certain linguistic proofs are brought forward which seem to show that the Hebrew text underlies the Greek, and that certain renderings in the Greek may be due to a misread Hebrew original. The suspicion arises—one wishes that it could be verified—that the Hebrew text may be a descendant of the lost original of Matthew's Gospel.

While unable to arrive at more definite conclusions as to the antecedents of this interesting Hebrew version, the writer feels convinced that it may worthily rank with other ancient versions, and that scholars will now be able to quote the Old Hebrew alongside the Old Latin and Old Syriac among their witnesses to the Sacred Text.

NOTE ON CHAPTER I

The following is a list, compiled by Dr. Herbst, of the principal scholars who have referred in their works to one or both of the Hebrew versions of Matthew's Gospel, published by S. Münster and J. du Tillet respectively:

Pagninus, *Thesaurus Linguæ Sanctæ*, 1614.

Dan. Chamier, *Panstrat. Cathol.*, Geneva, 1626.

Johannes-Baptista Jonas, *The Four Gospels in Hebrew*, Rome, 1668.

J. Chr. Wagenseil, *Sota*, Altdorf, 1674.

Polus, *Synopsis Crit.*, Frankfurt-a-Main, 1678.

P. D. Huet, *de interpretatione*, Stade, 1680.

R. Simon, *Hist. Crit. des Versions du Nouveau Testament*, Rotterdam, 1690.

Hugo Grotius, *Annotationes in Libros Evang.*, Amsterdam, 1691.

L. de Dieu, *Comment. in Matt.* (Critica Sacra), Amsterdam, 1693.

J. Mill, *Proleg. in Novum Testamentum*, Oxford, 1707.

Le Long, *Critica Sacra*, Paris, 1723.

Wetstein, *Proleg. ad Novum Testamentum*, Amsterdam, 1730.

J. G. Hagemann, *Historische Nachricht von den canonischen und apocryphischen Schriften des Alten und Neuen Testaments*, Braunschweig, 1748.

E. Chr. Schroedter, *Disput. phil. de lingua authentica Matthæi* (no date).

J. D. Michælis, *Einleitung in die göttlichen Schriften des Neuen Bundes* (no date).

J. H. Hottinger, *Thesaurus Philologicus* (no date).

CHAPTER II

SOME INTERESTING READINGS

It has already been remarked that the true origin of the Hebrew Matthew must largely be decided on the results obtained by an examination of the variant readings found in the text. Some of the more interesting of these are therefore discussed in the following pages. While forced through lack of material to refrain from making a complete survey of the variants, the writer hopes that the little light he has been able to throw on certain passages will make it worth the while of scholars to take the matter up seriously, and provide for the general reader a greater insight into some of the features of the First Gospel.

The Genealogy (Matt. 1 : 1–17)

The first point of interest lies in the Genealogy. The Hebrew text begins a new section at verse 3, obviously in order to draw special attention to the tribe of Judah from which the Messiah was descended. This at once calls to mind the words of the writer to the Hebrews (7 : 14) : " For it is evident that our Lord sprang out of Judah." Prior to the birth of Christ, a large body of Jewish opinion had been seeking to transfer the Messianic rôle to the tribe of Levi, believing that in the Maccabean priest-kings, especially in the person of John Hyrcanus, they had found the true saviour of the Jewish people. The Maccabees assumed the title of " priests of the Most High God," and it is believed by scholars, not without warrant, that the 110th Psalm, which speaks of the priest after the order of Melchizedek, was written in honour either of Simon Maccabæus or John Hyrcanus. Those who wish to pursue this subject further should read Dr. R. H. Charles' introduction to his translation of the *Testaments of the Twelve Patriarchs*. It need only be remarked here that it seems evident that the Genealogy and the Epistle to the Hebrews both protest against the false ascription of Messianic honours to the Maccabees, and point to Jesus as the true King of the line of David and Judah, while by virtue of His self-sacrifice he is High Priest also. Of much more importance, however, is verse 13, where a new name is added to the Genealogy. The Hebrew text here reads, " Abihud begat Abner ; Abner begat Eliakim " ; אביהוד הוליד את אבנר אבנר הוליד את אליקים. There can be no doubt from verse 17 that the compiler intended to divide his list into three groups of fourteen names each. It is not a little surprising, then, to discover on counting up the names that, while the first two groups have their complete complement of fourteen, the third group contains only thirteen names. A table will make this clear :

GROUP 1	GROUP 2	GROUP 3
1. Abraham.	1. Solomon.	1. Shealtiel.
2. Isaac.	2. Rehoboam.	2. Zerubbabel.
3. Jacob.	3. Abijam.	3. Abihud.
4. Judah.	4. Asa.	———
5. Pharez.	5. Jehoshaphat.	4. Eliakim.
6. Hezron.	6. Joram.	5. Azzur.
7. Ram.	7. Uzziah.	6. Zadok.
8. Amminadab.	8. Jotham.	7. Ammon.
9. Nahshon.	9. Ahaz.	8. Elihud.
10. Salmon.	10. Hezekiah.	9. Eleazer.
11. Boaz.	11. Menasseh.	10. Mattan.
12. Obed.	12. Ammon.	11. Jacob.
13. Jesse.	13. Josiah.	12. Joseph.
14. David.	14. Jeconiah.	13. Jesus.

Commentators have attempted to evade the difficulty by repeating the name of David at the head of Group 2, or that of Jeconiah at the head of Group 3. It is obvious, however, that a name is missing, and it would greatly influence opinion on the antiquity of the Hebrew text if it could be shown that the restored name of Abner is the correct one. One way of testing this point is to show good reason why it should have dropped out of the particular place where it is found in the Hebrew. Fortunately such a reason is not difficult to find, and the writer hazards, therefore, what appears to him a possible solution. On turning to other MS. authorities, the Old Syriac Gospels, Curetonian and Sinaitic, both read the name immediately preceding the name Abner in the Hebrew as Abiur, the difference between which and the form Abiud is very slight, the only alteration to be made being in the position of the dot on the last letter. In Hebrew the difference would be equally slight :

אביוד, Abiud.

אביור, Abiur.

Now the name Abner is sometimes written as אבינר, Abiner (cf. 1 Sam. 14 : 50, 51). Supposing the scribe to have had before him אביוד הוליד את אבינר, " Abiud begat Abiner," he might easily omit the second name as a dittograph, the נ, Nun, and ו,

Vaw, being readily confused in Hebrew though not in Syriac. Another variant in verse 14 may be similarly explained on the basis of a Hebrew original. Here we find the name Achim read as אמון, Ammon, where the Old Syriac has אכין, Achin. When it is remembered that the letter י, Yod, was often written with a long tail like a ו, Vaw, the difference between the Hebrew and Syriac is hardly distinguishable.

Other Variants due to a Hebrew Original [1]

Several other instances occur where a variant seems capable of solution on linguistic grounds, and these we may notice here.

Matt. 4 : 24—" and the report of him went out unto all the people." The entire clause is omitted by the Sinaitic Syriac,

---

[1] On the question of a Hebrew original, Margoliouth has an interesting remark. He says: " Further evidence that the original language of the Gospel in this chapter (I.) was not Syriac is to be found in verse 21, ' thou shalt call his name Jesus,' etc. Since the root to which the name Jesus belongs is not found in Syriac at all, had Syriac been the original language, it is reasonable to suppose that the Hebrew word would have been elucidated " (" The Matthæan Narrative of the Nativity," *Expositor*, Oct. 1919). Our Hebrew text is a confirmation of this statement, for we read, " Thou shalt call his name Jesus, ישוע : for he shall save—יושיע—his people from all their sins."

while the Greek MSS. read " throughout all Syria." We would suggest that הֶעָם, " the people," has been altered into ארם, " Aram (Syria)." The alteration may have been influenced by the wording of the letter reputed to have been written to Jesus by Abgar, the Syrian prince of Edessa, commencing, " I have heard the reports respecting thee, and thy cures——" The omission of the clause in the Sinaitic Syriac would then be due to homoioteleuton, as the word " people " concludes the preceding clause in verse 23.

Matt. 14 : 20—" and there were left over unto them twelve baskets full of the fragments." Compare this with the Greek : " and they took up of the fragments that remained twelve baskets full." Some confusion appears to have arisen between ונשארו, " and there were left over," and ונשאו, " and they took up." Similarly in Matt. 17 : 12 (last clause) the Hebrew has יקבל, " receive," which the Greek translator appears to have read as יסבל, " suffer."

Finally, we would draw attention to a new rendering of the cry from the Cross, Matt. 27 : 46, which is given in the Hebrew as אלי אלי למה שכחתני : " My God, my God, why hast thou forgotten me ? " instead of the usual rendering, " why hast thou forsaken me ? " It is common knowledge that the quotation as it stands in the Greek is a mixture of Hebrew and Aramaic, though Mark gives it entirely in Aramaic. We have evidence in Codex Bezæ and the Old Latin MSS. which read Zapthani, of early attempts to restore the text to the form in which it is found in the Hebrew of Ps. 22 : 1. But the problem admits of another solution. The new Hebrew rendering is obviously a combination of Ps. 22 : 1 with Ps. 42 : 9. In the latter passage we read, " I will say unto God my Rock, למה שכחתני, why hast thou forgotten me ? " Any one may see how closely the subject-matter of the two Psalms is related. The problem thus resolves itself into a choice between the Hebrew, שכחתני, and the Aramaic, שבקתני. May not both readings be due to the uncertain hearing of the eye-witnesses ? It must not be forgotten that some thought that He called for Elijah (Matt. 27 : 47).

THE BOOK OF JAMES

One of the earliest accounts of the infancy of Jesus containing important traditional matter was the *Book of James*. It was already current in Palestine in the first half of the second century, and was made use of by Justin Martyr. We have now to record some readings which are supported by this ancient document.

Matt. 1 : 19—" Now Joseph her husband was a just man, and not willing to deliver her up to death, nor to disclose her." Compare with this the *Book of James*, para. 14 : " and if I expose her to the sons of Israel . . . I shall be found delivering up innocent blood to the doom of death." [1]

Matt. 2 : 1—" Now after Jesus was born in Beth-lehem, a city of Judah," בעיר יהודה. Cf. Luke 1 : 39, 40—" And Mary arose in those days, and went into the hill country with haste, into a city of Judah εἰς πόλιν Ἰούδα ; and entered into the house of Zacharias and saluted Elisabeth."

---

[1] Here and elsewhere in this chapter it may be useful to the student to quote from the Commentaries of the Syrian Isho'dad of Merv on the Gospels, translated into English by Mrs. Gibson (Camb. Univ. Press). This important writer, who flourished *c.* A.D. 850, preserves for us many valuable traditions from early Christian sources, and it was with no little satisfaction that the present writer found that some of these confirmed variants in the Hebrew Text. *Ish. Comm.* on Matt. 1 : 19. " Nevertheless Joseph was just and merciful . . . for his justice oppressed him, that he should not allow an adulteress within his house ; and his mercy counselled him, that he should send her away privily ; because he knew that he would deliver her to death, if he exposed her," etc.

According to what we read in the *Book of
James*, para. 22, the house of Zacharias was in
Beth-lehem, from whence Elisabeth escaped
with John into the hill country to save him
from the massacre of the infants. The
mysterious city of Judah of Luke thus turns
out to be not a misread Juttah but a re-
ference to Beth-lehem. The combined testimony of the Hebrew text and the *Book of
James* is decisive.[1]

Matt. 2 : 12—" And it came to pass that
when they were fast asleep, behold, the
angel appeared unto them, saying, Beware
of returning to Jerusalem to Herod, so they
went and returned to their own country by
another way." In the *Book of James*, para.
21, this passage runs : " And having been
warned by the angel not to go into Judæa,
they went into their own country by another way." The *Gospel of pseudo-Matthew*
is even nearer : " And when they were going
to return to King Herod, they were warned
by an angel in their sleep not to go back to

[1] *Ish. Comm.*, p. 7 : " Priests were killed because of David,
and children because of our Lord. Abiathar escaped from
among the priests, and John from among the children." P. 22 :
" But how was John removed ? Mar Ephraim and others say
that Elisabeth withdrew him from before the sword of Herod."
P. 23 : " Others say that when Zacharias his father felt the
sword of Herod, perhaps the boy was sought ; for he was from
the border of Bethlehem."

Herod ; and they returned to their own country by another way."

HARMONISATION WITH LUKE

One of the striking peculiarities of early Gospel quotations, whether in the Fathers, or the apocryphal Gospels, or in such writings as the *Didaché*, is the harmonisation which is often to be found, especially between Matthew and Luke. We must suppose that originally the texts of these two Gospels approximated much more closely to each other than they do now, or else that at a very early date attempts were made to make them so. Probably there is truth in both assertions ; as witness the popularity of Tatian's harmony, the *Diatessaron.* There are a considerable number of such harmonised passages in our Hebrew text which the reader will easily find in going through the translation ; but we may select a few examples for illustration here :

MATT. 5 : 44 (Gr.)	MATT. 5 : 44 (Heb.)	LUKE 6 : 27, 28
But I say unto you, Love your enemies (bless them that curse you, do good to them that hate you), and pray for them which (despitefully use you and) persecute you.	But I say unto you, Love your enemies, do good to them that hate you, and pray for them that persecute you and despitefully use you.	But I say unto you which hear, Love your enemies, do good to them that hate you, bless them that curse you, and pray for them which despitefully use you.

The bracketed sections in the Greek text are omitted in most MSS., which makes the agreement between the Hebrew and Luke more marked. Justin Martyr (*Apol.* 1 : 15) also quotes the passage in a form nearer to Luke, and the *Didaché* (1 : 3) practically agrees with Justin. The Vulgate is identical with the Hebrew.

MATT. 7 : 1, 2 (Gr.)	MATT. 7 : 1, 2 (Heb.)	LUKE 6 : 37, 38
Judge not, that ye be not judged.	*A.* Judge not, and ye shall not be judged.	Judge not, and ye shall not be judged.
	B. Condemn not, and ye shall not be condemned.	Condemn not, and ye shall not be condemned.
For with what judgment ye judge, ye shall be judged :	*A.* For with what judgment ye judge, ye shall be judged :	(. . . .
		. . . .)
And with what measure ye mete, it shall be measured unto you again.	*B.* And with what measure ye mete, it shall be measured unto you again.	For with the same measure ye mete withal, it shall be measured unto you again.

The Hebrew text is a perfect specimen of parallelism, lost by omission in the Greek Matthew and expansion in Luke. At a very early date we have a crowding of precepts into this passage, *e.g.* in the epistles of Clement of Rome and Polycarp.

Matt. 18 : 12 (Heb.)—" doth he not leave the ninety and nine sheep in the wilderness ? " (Cf. Luke 15 : 4.)

Matt. 24 : 41 (Heb.)—" Two (men) shall be in one bed ; one shall be taken, and one shall be left." (Cf. Luke 17 : 36.)

Both these readings are found in the earlier editions of the Vulgate : the latter seems also to have been the reading in Isho'dad's copy. (*Ish. Comm.* in Matt. 24.)

PLACE NAMES

Matt. 26 : 36—For " Gethsemane " the Hebrew reads " Ge-shemanim," גי שמנים, as in Isa. 28 : 1, where it is rendered " the fat valley." The reading of the Old Syriac " Gu-semani " and some Greek MSS., γησαμανει and γεσσημανει point to the same derivation.

Matt. 27 : 8—" The field of blood " in the Hebrew, " Chakel-damah—" חקל דמה—as in Acts 1 : 19. One Old Latin MS. of Matthew leaves the name untranslated.

Matt. 27 : 33 — " Golgotha " is spelt correctly in the Hebrew, " Golgoltha," and left without explanation, which was unnecessary.

Matt. 27 : 57—" Arimathæa," correctly spelt, " Ha-Ramathaim." (Cf. 1 Sam. 1 : 1.)

SOME OTHER READINGS

We cannot close this chapter without alluding to a few other variants found in the

Hebrew Gospel, though it would occupy far too much space to deal with them all. Many familiar incidents receive fresh illumination, while the touch of the Master is more keenly felt in the form given to many of his choicest utterances.

Matt. 1 : 20—At the end of this verse the Hebrew adds, " for of the Holy Spirit she has conceived." This reading, though not found elsewhere, receives some support from the text used by Justin Martyr. In the story of the annunciation the angel says to Mary, " Behold, thou shalt conceive of the Holy Spirit " (*Dial. with Trypho*, 33). In Luke, the text reads : " And, behold, thou shalt conceive in thy womb " (Luke 1 : 31). In the final clause of Matt. 1 : 20, in the A.V., the word conceived is rightly rendered in the margin begotten, and does not therefore enter into the discussion.

Matt. 2 : 23—" for he shall be called Nazareth." The new form of this testimony does not materially help forward its solution, which still remains a mystery. None of the ingenious explanations of commentators can minimise the direct force of the quotation. Both the Hebrew and the Old Syriac refer the saying to the " prophet " (sing.). The source may possibly be a lost

writing of Jeremiah. The question is of
some importance in connection with Matt.
27 : 9, where a prophecy is attributed to
Jeremiah which is no longer to be found in
his extant works. Jerome, who was very
familiar with the Judæo-Christians and
their literature, tells us that he " lately
read in a Hebrew book, which a Hebrew of
the Nazarene sect showed me, an apocryphon
of Jeremiah, in which I found this (prophecy),
word for word." [1] Such a volume in the
possession of the very community which
claimed to possess the original Hebrew of
Matthew's Gospel is surely significant. This
peculiar regard for Jeremiah [2] finds a further
echo in the Hebrew of Matt. 2 : 17, where,
after the name of the prophet, the benedic-
tion " upon whom be peace " [3] is inserted.

Matt. 5 : 46—In this place and throughout

[1] James, *The Lost Apocrypha of the Old Testament*, p. 62.

[2] In the second book of Maccabees we read how Judas saw in
a dream " a man appear, of venerable age and exceeding glory,
and wonderful and most majestic was the dignity around him :
and Onias answered and said, This is the lover of the brethren,
he who prayeth much for the people and the holy city, Jeremiah,
the prophet of God : and Jeremiah, stretching forth his right
hand, delivered to Judas a sword of gold, and in giving it ad-
dressed him thus, Take the holy sword, a gift from God, wherewith thou shalt smite down the adversaries " (15 : 13–16).

[3] Compare the same phrase in the so-called fifth book of
Maccabees : " Daniel the prophet (upon whom be peace) "
(12 : 1) ; " the sons of David (upon whom be peace) " (21 : 17).

the Gospel the Hebrew has transgressors
(בעלי עברה) for publicans (τελῶναι). This
appears to be the true reading on the following grounds : (1) The parties in question
are commonly associated with sinners, ἁμαρ-
τωλοί (Heb. חטאים), 9 : 10 ; 11 : 19, or harlots,
21 : 31. Now, if tax-gatherers are intended,
it is curious to find them singled out for
classification with such company. Why not
dicers, usurers, or members of some other
immoral profession ? If, however, we accept
the word transgressors we find the conjunc-
tion to be an ordinary Jewish usage : thus
we get such associations as these—" the
wicked (Sept. ' ungodly ') and the sinner "
(Prov. 11 : 31) ; " the ungodly and the
sinner " (1 Pet. 4 : 18) ; " sinners and ungodly " (Enoch 38 : 3) ; " sinners and evil-
doers " (ibid. 45 : 5). (2) עבר is often used
in the O.T. in speaking of transgressing
the law, covenant, or commandments of God
(Deut. 26 : 13 ; Josh. 7 : 11 ; Dan. 9 : 11,
etc.), and in the N.T. we have the Greek
equivalent, " a transgressor of the law,"
παραβάτης νόμου (Jas. 2 : 11) ; " Why do ye
also transgress, παραβαίνετε (Heb. עוברים),
the commandment of God ? " (Matt. 15 : 3).
(3) At the time of Christ this very term,
" transgressors," was used to denote a class

3

of people who might fitly be grouped with sinners, harlots, and heathen.[1]

Matt. 7 : 21—" Not every one that saith unto me, Lord, lord, shall enter into the kingdom of Heaven; but he that doeth the will of my Father which is in heaven, the same shall enter with me into the kingdom of Heaven." The last clause, except for the words " with me," is also found in the Vulgate and Curetonian Syriac. This variant occurs again in the Hebrew of Matt. 10 : 37, which reads : " and whoso loveth son or daughter more than me is not worthy to be with me in the kingdom of Heaven." (Cf. Matt. 26 : 29, Luke 23 : 43, John 17 : 24.)

Matt. 8 : 20 — " The foxes have holes,

---

[1] " As in most countries of some degree of culture where many of the inhabitants have attained to means and even to wealth, so also in Palestine there were the superior ' breakers of the yoke,' scoffers and doubters, seeking only after pleasure and dissipation.   Of such a type especially were the great landed proprietors, the rich men and merchants, certain members of the high priestly families, and most of the royal families who were in contact with the Greeks and Romans.   It was in Jerusalem, the centre of culture and the home of the richer and ruling classes, where were to be found the greatest number of these ' wicked ' and ' ungodly,' who ' kicked ' owing to excessive prosperity, and oppressed the poorer and weaker classes. . . . Likewise among the *Am-ha-aretz* (unlearned) were to be found ' breakers of the yoke,' who were such owing to their boorishness, ignorance and dissoluteness, and these were known by the name עבריינים, ' transgressors ' " (Dr. J. Klausner, *Jesus of Nazareth*, p. 196).

and the birds of the heavens nests ; but the son of Man hath not a floor whereon he may lay his head." The addition of the word קרקע, floor, gives a new pathos to this utterance, which seems to refer to accommodation in the common khan or caravanserai of the village, where the rudest provision was made for the traveller in the allotment of a paved recess, raised a foot or two above the level of the courtyard where the cattle were tied. Such travellers " would neither expect nor require attendance, and would pay only the merest trifle for the advantage of shelter, safety, and a floor on which to lie." [1]

Matt. 11 : 2—The use of the Hebrew, בית הסוחר, a fortified prison, or castle, to describe the place of John's confinement is in agreement with Josephus, who states that John was imprisoned in the fortress of Macherus (cf. *Wars*, VII. vi. 2, *Antiq.* XVIII. v. 2).

Matt. 11 : 19 — " And the Son of Man came both eating and drinking, and they say, Behold, the man, a glutton and a drunkard, and a friend of transgressors and sinners." These words show that Jesus was denounced by some as a " stubborn and

[1] Farrar, *Life of Christ*, p. 4.

rebellious son," according to Deut. 21 : 18–21, Prov. 23 : 19–25.

Matt. 11 : 29—" Take my yoke upon you, and learn of me ; for I am driven out and downcast in spirit : and ye shall find rest for your souls." Some may be inclined to take exception to this rendering of a time-honoured text, but there is no doubt that Jesus is using the language of the farmer. The last clause is a direct quotation of Jer. 6 : 16, and may be compared with Ps. 23 : 3 ; while the Hebrew word נער, driven out, is used of cattle in Zech. 11 : 16.

Matt. 13 : 55—" Is he not the smith's son ? " So also the Vulgate.

Matt. 14 : 4—" For she said unto him, Jochanan is not worthy to be with thee." According to this rendering, Herodias was jealous of John's influence over Herod. (Cf. Mark 6 : 19, 20.)

Matt. 17 : 2—" And his face was trans-figured before them." This clause is quoted because of its use of a very rare Hebrew word, which solves a long-standing problem of the Old Testament. In Josh. 9 : 4 we read that the Gibeonites " made as if they had been ambassadors," while the Revised Version (margin) gives " took them pro-visions," as in verse 12. The Hebrew word, of which these are attempted translations, is יצטיררו, the third person plural, Hithpæl, of the root ציר, to twist or turn. The true translation is now made clear by the use of the identical form of this verb in the sense of transfigure. Josh. 9 : 4 should therefore be corrected to " they transformed [or disguised] themselves."

Matt. 19 : 28—For " in the regeneration " the Hebrew reads " in the second birth " (cf. John 3 : 3). As the Resurrection is the second birth, so the Judgment is the second death (Rev. 20 : 14).

Matt. 22 : 43—" How then doth David by his holy spirit call him Lord." The expression, " his holy spirit," may strike the reader as somewhat strange, but it has many parallels in ancient Jewish literature. In the apocryphal *History of Susanna* we read : " God raised up the holy spirit of a young youth, whose name was Daniel " (verse 45). Again, in the Zadokite document, translated by Dr. Charles, the phrase occurs twice : " They also polluted their holy spirit" (7 : 12) ; " And no man shall make abominable his holy spirit " (8 : 20). Dr. Charles quotes in explanation the Hebrew *Testament of Naphtali* (10 : 9) : " Blessed is the man who does not defile the holy spirit of God which hath been put and breathed unto him." The holy spirit thus in a sense corresponds to the soul. Acts 17 : 16 in a Hebrew original would probably have read : " Now while Paul waited for them at Athens, his holy spirit was stirred within him, when he saw the city full of idols."

In Matt. 24 : 32 there is a clear case of a play on words which points distinctly to a Hebrew original. The word translated summer in the Authorised Version is in the Hebrew text קיץ (ripe fruit), while the " it is near " of verse 33 refers to the " end " (verse 14), in Hebrew, קץ. The same play on the two Hebrew words is found in Amos 8 : 2—" And he said, Amos, what seest thou ? And I said, A basket of ripe fruit (קיץ). Then said the Lord unto me, The end (קץ) is come upon my people of Israel," etc.

Matt. 27 : 5—" (Judas) hanged himself with a halter." This account is also found in the Vulgate and in one MS. of the *Acts of Pilate*.[1]

In Matt. 27 : 26–27 we find Pilate hand-

---

[1] *Ish. Comm.*, p. 110 : " But at the same time, that it might not be supposed by many that the disciples had killed him, but he escaped, either the rope being cut by the act of God, or else some one perceived him, and saved him from strangulation ; and in the midst of the streets he burst asunder, as Luke wrote in the Acts, and his bowels gushed out."

ing Jesus over to the Jewish authorities who carry out the scourging and crucifixion. This account is certainly the correct one : it is vouched for by Luke, John, the Acts and the apocryphal *Gospel of Peter*, etc. Although the Jewish authorities at this period had to gain the consent of the Roman Governor, upon whom the responsibility really rested, before putting any man to death, there was nothing to prevent them carrying out the execution once that consent had been obtained. The fact that the sentence was for death by crucifixion proves no more than that Jesus was condemned on political rather than religious grounds. To say that Jews crucified Christ is very different from saying that the Jews crucified Him. A very real distinction must be drawn between those traitors to Judaism, the sycophantic chief priests and their adherents, and the patriotic Jewish populace whom they feared and tyrannised over. That the actual execution was carried out by the hands of Roman soldiers only heightens the tragedy of the blow struck by Jews at the very heart of Jewish liberty, for which Christ died a martyr.

The writer would gladly have given space to further reflections arising out of a con-

sideration of the Hebrew text, and it is
hoped that in going through the translation
the reader will take note of other interesting differences by comparing it with the
Authorised Version. The principal aim of
this chapter has been to give special pro-
minence to readings calculated to influence
a decision on the antiquity of the Hebrew
Gospel. We have seen how in the matter
of language and local colour there are
variants which cannot be reconciled with a
date later than the second century A.D.,
while the parallelisms with the *Book of
James,* which cannot be accidental, point
to the same early date. Further confirmatory evidence is supplied by the harmonisa-
tions with Luke's Gospel, a tendency more
prominent in the second century than at
any other period, and the support afforded
to some readings by Western authorities
such as the Old Latin and Old Syriac Gospels,
and Justin Martyr, also suggest the second
century. The cumulative effect of these
testimonies is very convincing, and seems
to show that in the Hebrew Gospel there
have survived genuine elements of the sub-
apostolic age.

TABLE OF READINGS IN COMMON WITH THE OLD SYRIAC (CURETONIAN AND SINAITIC) GOSPELS

I.

6. David begat Solomon. *11. in the Babylonian Exile.
*20. fear not to take Miriam.
21. that which shall be born of her is of the Holy Spirit, for of the Holy Spirit she has conceived. (Heb.) that which shall be born of her is conceived of the Holy Spirit. (Cur.) 22. Isaiah the prophet.

II.

*7. appeared unto them. 23. the prophet.

III.

5. from Jerusalem.
*9. And say not among yourselves.
15. and immersed him. 16. as the likeness of a dove.

IV.

*3. saith unto him. 4. Jesus answered.
5. turret of the Temple. 17. to preach saying.
18. Kepha.

V.

22. whosoever shall say to·him (. . . to his brother. Cur.)
45. on the good and on the evil.
*47. Gentiles.

VI.

11. our continual bread.

VII.

*4. Suffer it now.
*21. shall enter . . . into the kingdom of Heaven.
22. mighty works. *29. scribes and Pharisees.

VIII.

18. he commanded his disciples.
*31. send us into the herd of swine.

IX.

*13. (omit) to repentance.
*28. Yea, of a truth, Lord. (Yea, we believe, Lord. Sin.)

X.

*8. raise the dead, cleanse the lepers.

XI.

5. the poor are made happy (. . . are sustained. Cur.)
11. he that is little in the kingdom of Heaven.

XII.

*15. and many followed him.
*46. to the crowd.
*46. and were seeking to speak with him.
50. my brethren, and my sisters, and my mother.

XIII.

5. fell upon the rock.   *36. Then he.
*44. (omit) Again.   *48. chose the good.
*51. (omit) Jesus saith unto them.
*51. (omit) Lord.

XV.

*1. Then drew nigh unto him.
22. (omit) unto him.   *30. at his feet.
32. and saith unto them.

XVI.

*13. Whom do the children of men say that the Son of
     Man is ? (Heb.)
     What do men say concerning me ? who then is this
     Son of Man ? (Syr.)

XVII.

*2. white as the snow.
*18. And Jesus rebuked him ; and the demon went out of him.
 20. And he . . . saith.   *26. And he said.

XVIII.

*6. upper millstone (lit. ass millstone).
*10. their angels in heaven.
*12. and goeth and seeketh that which is lost.
*29. (omit) at his feet.

XIX.

*3. (omit) unto him.
 5. his father and his mother.
 14. theirs is the kingdom of Heaven.
 16. that I may inherit.
*17. Why askest thou me concerning the good ?
*24. kingdom of Heaven.

XX.

*6. (omit) idle.   *7. my vineyard.
*7. (omit) and whatsoever is right, that shall ye receive.
*17. his twelve disciples.   *23. to give you.
 30. (omit) O Lord.
*34. and immediately they saw.

XXI.

*1. two of his disciples.   27. he also said.
 37. Perhaps they will reverence my son.
*38. his inheritance will be ours.

XXII.

 7. burned with fire.   16. the servants of Herod.
 18. said unto them.   37. and with all thy might.
 42. Son of David.

XXIII.

*19. (omit) fools.   *25. and uncleanness.
28. depravity and violence.

XXIV.

*2. But he answered.   *27. and is visible.

XXV.

*2. Five of them were foolish, and five of them were
    prudent.

XXVI.

36. Ge-Shemanim (Gusemani.   Sin.)
53. ask of the Father.

XXVII.

*4. the blood of the righteous.
13. the witness which they witness (how many witnesses
    witness.   Sin.)
*26. delivered Jesus to them.
33. Golgoltha.
33. (omit) that is to say, a place of a skull.
*34. gave him wine.   43. if he desire.
46. (omitting the interpretation of the cry.)

XXVIII.

*1. And on the evening of the Sabbath.
*3. His appearance.   *3. (omit) white.

Of these ninety-five agreements with the Old Syriac, fifty-three (marked with an asterisk) also agree with the Vulgate. This is sufficient to prove that the Hebrew text no more depends on the Vulgate than do the Old Syriac Gospels.

PART II

TRANSLATION OF THE TEXT

NOTES ON THE TRANSLATION

As far as it was consistent with accurate
translation, the English of the Authorised
Version has been followed. The text has
been divided into chapters and paragraphs
as in the Hebrew, the corresponding verses
of the English Bible being put in the margin.

The translator has not deemed it necessary
to reproduce the full Hebrew text, as both
the 1555 and 1879 editions are accessible
to scholars. For the same reason, no
attempt has been made to quote the various
MS. authorities for and against particular
readings, which would have been out of
place in a popular work.

In order, however, that the interested
reader may have the opportunity of judging
of the original text and the accuracy of the
translation, the Hebrew of the more un-
common words and expressions, together
with the principal variants, and the Old
Testament quotations in full, have been
added as footnotes.

Personal and place names have been left

in their Jewish forms, except foreign names, such as Herod, Archelaus, Pilate, etc., and the name Jesus, too familiar and beloved to alter, though in the Hebrew it is written as Jeshu, and sometimes in the fuller form, Jeshua.

THE GOSPEL OF MATTHEW

1 1 These are the genealogies of Jesus, the son of David,[1] the son of Abraham.
2 Abraham begat Isaac ; Isaac begat Jacob ; Jacob begat Judah and his brethren.
3 Judah begat Pharez and Zerah of Tamar ; Pharez begat Hezron ; Hezron
4 begat Ram ; and Ram begat Amminadab ; Amminadab begat Nahshon ;
5 Nahshon begat Salmon ; Salmon begat Boaz of Rahab ; Boaz begat Obed of Ruth ; and Obed begat Jesse ;
6 Jesse begat David the king ; and David begat Solomon of the wife of
7 Uriah ; and Solomon begat Rehoboam ; Rehoboam begat Abijam ;
8 and Abijam begat Asa ; and Asa begat Jehoshaphat ; Jehoshaphat begat
9 Joram ; Joram begat Uzziah ; Uzziah begat Jotham ; Jotham begat Ahaz ;
10 Ahaz begat Hezekiah ; Hezekiah begat Menasseh ; Menasseh begat Ammon ;

¹אלה תולדות ישו בן דוד.

4

11 Ammon begat Josiah ; Josiah begat Jeconiah and his brethren in the
12 Babylonian Exile. Jeconiah begat Shealtiel ; Shealtiel begat Zerubbabel ;
13 Zerubbabel begat Abihud ; Abihud begat Abner ; [1] Abner begat Eliakim ;
14 Eliakim begat Azzur ; Azzur begat Zadok ; Zadok begat Ammon ; Ammon
15 begat Elihud ; Elihud begat Eleazar ; Eleazar begat Mattan ; Mattan begat
16 Jacob ; Jacob begat Joseph the husband of Miriam, of whom was born
17 Jesus, who is called Messiah. So all the generations from Abraham to David are fourteen generations . . . [2] and from the Babylonian Exile to the
18 Messiah are fourteen generations. Now the birth of Jesus the Messiah was on this wise : After his mother Miriam was betrothed to Joseph, before he came unto her, she was found with
19 child of the Holy Spirit. Now Joseph her husband was a just man, and was not willing to deliver her up to death, nor to disclose her ; [3] only it was in his heart to send her away privily.

[1] אביהוד הוליד את אבנר.

[2] There is probably a lacuna here.

[3] ולא אבה למסור אותה למיתה ולא לגלותה. (Cf. *Bk. of James.*)

20 But while he thought on this, the
angel appeared unto him in a dream,
saying, Joseph, thou son of David,
fear not to take Miriam thy wife,
because that which shall be born of
her is of the Holy Spirit (for of the
Holy Spirit she is with child).[1]
21 And, behold, she shall bring forth a
son, and thou shalt call his name
Jesus ; for he shall save his people
22 from all their sins. And all this
was to fulfil what was spoken of the
Lord[2] by the prophet Isaiah, saying,
23 Behold, the maiden is with child,
and shall bring forth a son, and shall
24 call his name Immanuel.[3] Then
Joseph awoke from his sleep, and
did as the angel of the Lord had
commanded him, and took her as
25 his wife : but he knew her not till
she had brought forth her son, the
firstborn : and he called his name
Jesus.

[1] כי מרוח הקדש היא הרה.

[2] The representation of the tetragrammaton with three yods
,׳, found throughout the Hebrew text is similarly depicted in
the Hebrew *Wisdom of Ben Sira*, and other Hebrew documents. (See *The Wisdom of Ben Sira*, edited by Schechter
and Taylor, Cambridge, 1899, Introduction, p. 8.)

[3] הנה העלמה הרה ויולדת בן וקראת שמו עמנואל. (Isa. 7 : 14.)

2 1 Now after Jesus was born in Bethlehem, a city of Judah,[1] in the days of Herod the king, behold, there came magicians [2] from the east to Jeru-

2 salem, saying, Where is he that is born king of the Jews ? for we have seen his star in the east, and are come to

3 do him homage. And when Herod heard, he was filled with wrath,[3] both he, and all Jerusalem with him.

4 And when he had gathered all the chief priests and scribes of the people together, he demanded of them in what place the Messiah should be

5 born. And they said unto him, In Beth-lehem-Judah : for thus it was spoken by the mouth of the prophet.

6 And thou Beth-lehem-Ephrathah, art not to be lightly esteemed among the thousands of Judah : from thee shall he come forth unto me, which is to be ruler among my people Israel.[4]

7 Then Herod called the magicians privily, and questioned them exactly [5]

¹ בעיר יהודה.

² מכשפים.   ³ נתמלא חמה.

⁴ ואתה בית לחם אפרתה לא צעיר להיות באלפי יהודה ממד לי יצא להיות מושל בעמי ישראל.   (Mic. 5 : 2.)

⁵ וחקר מהם היטב.

as to the time of the star, which had appeared unto them.

8 And he sent them to Beth-lehem, and said, Go and search diligently for the boy ; and when ye have found him, tell me, in order that I may come

9 and do him homage also. And when they had heard the king, they went their way ; and, behold, the star, which they saw in the east, went before their eyes, till it came and stood still above, over against where

10 the boy was. And when they saw the star, they rejoiced with exceeding

11 great joy. And when they were come into the house, they found the boy, and his mother, Miriam, with him, and they fell upon the ground and did him homage : and when they had opened their stores, they presented unto him gifts ; gold, and frankincense,

12 and myrrh. And it came to pass, when they were fast asleep, behold, the angel appeared unto them, saying, Beware of returning to Jerusalem to Herod,[1] so they went and returned to their own country by another way.

---

¹ ויהי הם אחוזים בשנה והנה המלאך נראה אליהם לאמר השמרו

משוב ירושלם אל הורודוס. (Cf. *Bk. of James.*)

13   And after they were departed, behold, the angel of the Lord appeared to Joseph in a dream, saying, Arise, take the boy and his mother, and flee thee away into Egypt and be there ; and there thou shalt stay until I return unto thee : for Herod is seeking to put the boy to death.

14 And he arose, and did as the angel had said unto him,[1] and took up the boy and his mother by night, and

15 departed into Egypt : and was there until the death of Herod : to fulfil what was spoken of the Lord by the prophet, he who said, Out of Egypt

16 have I called my son.[2]   Then Herod, seeing that he was deceived by the magicians, was exceedingly furious, and sent forth, and put to death all the boys that were in Beth-lehem, and in all the border thereof, from two years old and under, as he had heard the set time from the magicians.

17   Then was established that which was spoken by Jeremiah the prophet (upon

18 whom be peace),[3] who said, A voice

---

[1] ויעש כאשר אמר לו המלאך.
[2] ממצרים קראתי לבני.   (Hos. 11 : 1.)
[3] ירמיהו הנביא עליו השלום.

was heard in Ramah, lamentation and
bitter weeping, Rachel weeping for her
children, refusing to be comforted for
her children, because they are no more.[1]

19 But after Herod was dead, behold,
the angel of the Lord appeared in a
dream to Joseph in Egypt, saying,
20 Arise, take up the boy and his mother,
and go into the land of Israel : for
they are dead which sought the child's
21 life. Then he arose, and took the
child and his mother, and came into
22 the land of Israel. But when he
heard that Archelaus reigned in Judah
in the stead of Herod his father, he
was afraid to go thither : and being
warned in sleep, he went into the
23 land of Galilee : and came and dwelt
in the city of Nazareth : to fulfil
what was spoken by the mouth of the
prophet, For he shall be called
Nazareth.[2]

3 1 In those days Jochanan the immerser was called ; [3] and he cried in
2 the wilderness of Judah, saying, Re-

---

[1] קול ברמה נשמע נהי בכי תמרורים רחל מבכה על בניה מאנה
להנחם על בניה כי איננו. (Jer. 31 : 15.)

[2] כי נצרת יקרא.

[3] בימים ההם קרא ליוחנן המטביל. (Luke 3 : 2.)

pent ye of your lives,[1] for the kingdom of Heaven is nigh at hand.
3 And this is he of whom Isaiah spake,
saying, A voice crying in the wilderness, Prepare ye the way of the Lord,
make straight in the desert a high-
4 way for our God.[2] And the raiment
of Jochanan was of camel's hair, and
a leathern girdle about his loins ; and
his food was the locust and wild honey.[3]
5 Then went they out to him from
Jerusalem, and from Judah, and from
all the region of Jordan, and were
6 immersed of him in the Jordan,
7 confessing their sins. And when he
saw many of the Pharisees and Zadducees, which came to his immersion,
he said unto them, Generation of
vipers, who hath informed you to
8 flee from the wrath to come ? [4] Bring
forth therefore the fruit meet for
9 repentance : and say not among yourselves, Because Abraham is our
father : for I say unto you, that

[1] עשו תשובה בחיים.
[2] קול קורא במדבר פנו דרך י"י ישרו בערבה מסילה לאלהינ ו
(Isa. 40 : 3.)
[3] ארבה ודבש היער.   (Cf. I Sam. 14 : 27.)
[4] מי הודיעכם לברוח מן החרון הבא.

God has ability [1] to raise up the children
10 of Abraham from these stones.   And
already the axe is laid to the root
of the trees :   and every tree which
yieldeth not good fruit shall be cut
down, and cast into the fire.

11   I am only immersing you in water
unto repentance :   but he that cometh
after me is mightier than I, whose
sandals I am not worthy to carry :   and
he shall immerse you in the fire of the
12 Holy Spirit : [2] whose fan is in his
hand, that he may cleanse his floor,
and gather his wheat into the granary ;
but he will burn up the chaff with fire
unquenchable.

13   Then cometh Jesus from Galilee by
the Jordan unto Jochanan, that he
14 may   be   immersed   of   him.   But
Jochanan   spake   unto   him,   saying,
I have need to be immersed of thee,
15 and comest thou to me ?   Then Jesus
answered and saith unto him, Suffer
it now : [3] for in this it becometh us
to fulfil all righteousness.   He gave
16 him leave, and immersed him. [4]   Now
after Jesus was immersed and gone

² באש רוח הקדש. ¹ שיש יכולת בידי האלהים.

⁴ הניחו וטבלו. ³ הרף נא.

up out of the water, behold, the
heavens were opened unto him, and,
behold, the Spirit of God descending
from the heavens as the likeness of a
17 dove,[1] and coming upon him : and,
behold, out of the heavens a voice,
saying, This is my beloved Son, in
whom I am well pleased.[2]

4 1 Then Jesus was led up of the
Spirit into the wilderness of Judah [3]
in order that he may be tempted of
2 Satan. And when he had fasted
forty days and forty nights, there-
3 after he hungered. And when the
tempter came, he saith unto him, If
thou be the Son of God, command
that these stones be made bread.
4 But Jesus answered and saith, It is
written that, Not by bread alone
shall man live, but by whatsoever
proceedeth from the mouth of God
5 shall man live.[4] Then Satan taketh
him up into the holy city, and
setteth him on a turret of the

(Cf. *Gospel of the Hebrews*, ἐν εἴδει περιστερᾶς.) [1] .כדמות יונה

[2] .זה בני אהובי אשר בו רצתה נפשי

[3] .במדבר יהודה (Cf. Matt. 3 : 1.)

[4] לא על הלחם לבדו יחיה האדם כי על כל מוצא פי י׳י יחיה
האדם. (Deut. 8 : 3.)

6 Temple,[1] and saith unto him, If thou
be the Son of God, precipitate thyself
down : for surely it is written, For
he shall give his angels charge concerning thee, to keep thee in all thy
ways : upon the palms of their hands
they shall bear thee up, lest thou
dash thy foot against a stone.[2]   But

7 Jesus answered him and saith, It is
also written, Thou shalt not tempt

8 the Lord thy God.[3]   And again, Satan
taketh him up into an exceeding high
mountain, and sheweth him all the
kingdoms of the world, and their

9 glory ; and saith unto him, All these
will I give thee, if thou wilt fall down

10 and do me homage.   Then said Jesus
unto him, Get thee gone, Satan : for
it is written, The Lord thy God thou
shalt worship, and him alone thou

11 shalt serve.[4]   Then Satan left him,
and, behold, angels drew nigh and

12 ministered unto him.   Now after Jesus
had heard that Jochanan was taken

---

[1] פנת ההכל.   (Cf. 2 Chron. 26 : 15.)
[2] כי מלאכיו יצוה לך לשמרך בכל דרכיך על כפים ישאוך פן תגוף
באבן רגלך.   (Ps. 91 : 11, 12.)
[3] לא תנסה את י׳י אלוהיך.   (Deut. 6 : 16.)
[4] את י׳י אלהיך תשתחוה ואותו לבדו תעבוד.   (Deut. 6 : 13.)

13 prisoner, he went into Galilee ; and
   leaving Nazareth, he removed and
   dwelt in Kephar-Nahum (which is
   a city by the sea, on the border of
14 Zebulon and Naphtali) : to establish
   what was spoken by the mouth of
   Isaiah the prophet, who said, Land of
15 Zebulon, and land of Naphtali, the
   way of the sea, beyond Jordan, Galilee
16 of the Gentiles ; the people that
   walked in darkness have seen a great
   light ; the inhabitants of the land of
   the shadow of death, a light hath
17 shined upon them.[1] And then began
   Jesus to cry, saying, Turn ye, turn ye,
   in repentance : [2] for the kingdom of
   Heaven is nigh.

18 And when Jesus was walking by the
   sea of Galilee, he saw two brethren,
   Simeon who was called Kepha, and
   Andrew his brother, casting a net
   into the sea : for they were fishers.
19 And he saith unto them, Follow me,
   and I will make you fishers of men.
20 And they immediately left the nets, and

---

[1] ארצה זבלון וארצה נפתלי דרך הים עבר הירדן נליל הגוים העם
ההולכים בחושך ראו אור נדול יושבי בארץ צלמות אור ננה עליהם.
(Isa. 9 : 1, 2.)

[2] שובו שובו בתשובה.

21 followed him. And when he departed
thence, he saw two other brethren,
Jacob the son of Zabdi, and Jochanan
his brother, in a ship with Zabdi their
father, mending their nets ; and he
22 called them. And they immediately
left the ship and their father, and
followed him.

23   And Jesus went about all Galilee,[1]
teaching in their synagogues, and
announcing the kingdom, and healing
all manner of sickness and pain [2]
24 among the people. And the report
of him went forth unto all the people : [3]
and they brought unto him all that
had any bodily ill, or that were fallen
into divers sicknesses and diseases,
and such as were possessed of demons,
both epileptic and paralytic ; [4] and
he healed them.
25   And there followed him great
crowds [5] from Galilee, and from
Decapolis, and from Jerusalem, and
from Judah, and from beyond
Jordan.

[2] מכאוב.   [1] וילך ישוע סביב בכל גליל.
[3] ותצא שמועתו אל כל העם.
[4] בעלי שדים את הנופלים ואת נשולי אברים.
[5] כיתות רבות.

5 1 And when Jesus saw the crowds,
he went up into a mountain: and
after he had sat down, his disciples
2 approached him: and he opened his
mouth, and taught them, saying,
3 Happy are the poor in spirit:[1] for
theirs is the kingdom of Heaven.
4 Happy are they that mourn: for they
5 shall be comforted. Happy are the
meek: for they shall inherit the
6 earth. Happy are they which do
hunger and thirst for righteousness: for
7 they shall be filled. Happy are the
merciful: for they shall obtain mercy.
8 Happy are the pure in heart: for
9 they shall see God. Happy are the
peacemakers: for they shall be called
10 the children of God. Happy are they
which are persecuted for righteousness' sake: for theirs is the kingdom
11 of Heaven. Happy are ye, when men
shall revile you, and persecute you,
and shall say all manner of evil
against you falsely, for my sake.
12 Rejoice, and be glad: for great is
your reward in heaven: for so persecuted they the prophets which were
before you.

[1] עניי הרוח.

13   Ye are the salt of the earth : but
if the salt have lost its savour, wherewith shall it be salted ? it is thenceforth good for nothing, but to be cast
14 outside, and trampled of men.[1] Ye
are the light of the world. A city that
15 is set on a hill cannot be hid. Neither
do they obtain a lamp, to put it under
a measure,[2] but on a lampstand ; to
give light unto all that are in the
16 house. So let your light shine before
the children of men, in order that
they may see your good works, to
honour your Father which is in
heaven.

17   Think not that I am come to annul[3]
the Law or the Prophets : I am not
come to annul, but to fulfil.

18   Verily I say unto you, Till heaven
and earth pass away, one yod or one
hook[4] shall in no wise pass away
from the Law, till they all be ful-
19 filled.   And whosoever shall annul one
of these least commandments, and
shall teach the children of men so,
the same shall be called least in the
20 kingdom of Heaven.[5]   And I say unto

---

[4] עוקץ.   [3] לבטל.   [2] סאה   [1] וירמס מהאדם.
[5] Omitting last clause of verse 19.

you, Unless your righteousness exceed
the righteousness of the Pharisees and
scribes, ye shall not enter into the
21 kingdom of Heaven. Ye have heard
what was said to them of old time,[1]
Thou shalt not murder ; and whoso
committeth murder the same shall be
22 condemned to the judgment : but I
say unto you, That whosoever shall
be enraged against his brother,[2] the
same shall be condemned to the
judgment.

And whosoever saith unto his
brother, Thou evil one,[3] the same
shall be condemned to the council of
the synagogue.[4]

And whoso saith unto him, Thou
impious one,[5] the same shall be condemned to the fire of Gehinnom.

23   And if thou present thine offering
at the altar, and there rememberest
that thy brother hath ought against
24 thee ; leave there thine offering before
the altar, and go thou first to atone
to thy brother,[6] and then come and

---

[1] לקדמנים.
[2] מי שירגז על אחיו (omitting "without a cause.")
[3] רעה.   [4] חייב הוא לעצת הכנסת.
[5] נבל.   [6] לכפר את פני אחיך.

25 give thine offering. Come to terms [1]
with thine adversary speedily, whiles
thou art with him on the way ; lest
the adversary deliver thee up to the
judge, and the judge deliver thee up
to the officer, and thou be cast into
the gaol. [2]

26 Verily I say unto thee, Thou shalt
not go forth from thence, till thou
hast paid the last farthing.

27 Ye have heard that it was said to
them of old time, Thou shalt not
28 commit adultery : but I say unto
you, That whosoever seeth a woman
and lusteth for her hath already
committed adultery with her in his
29 heart. And if thy right eye offend
thee, [3] pluck it out, and cast it from
thee : for it is better for thee that
one of thy members should perish,
than that thy whole body should be
30 cast into Gehinnom. And if thy right
hand offend thee, cut it off, and cast
it from thee : for it is better for thee
that one of thy members should perish,
than that thy whole body should be
31 cast into Gehinnom. It was also said
concerning him that would put away

<hr>

³ תכשילך.   ² הכלא.   ¹ יאות.

5

his wife, that he should write her a bill
of divorcement, and give it unto her,
and send her away from his house:[1] but

32 I say unto you, That whosoever shall
put away his wife, saving for the cause
of fornication, causeth her to commit
adultery: and whosoever taketh her
that is cast off[2] committeth adultery.

33 Again, ye have heard that it was
said to them of old time, Thou shalt
not forswear thyself, but shalt pay

34 unto the Lord thy vow:[3] but I say
unto you, Ye shall not swear by
a confirming word;[4] neither by

35 heaven; for it is God's throne: nor
by the earth; for it is the footstool
of his feet; neither by Jerusalem;
for it is the city of the great king.

36 Neither shalt thou swear by thy head,
in that thou hast no power to whiten
one hair or to turn it black again.[5]

37 But let your words be, Yea, yea;
Nay, nay: for whatsoever is more
than these words is of evil.

¹ שיכתוב לה ספר כריתות ונתן לה ושלחה מביתו. ‏(‏.Deut. 24 : I‏)‏
² הגרושה.
³ לא תשבע לשקר כי אם תשלם לי״י נדרך.
⁴ בשום דבר.
⁵ יען שאין בידך כח להלבין שער אחד או להחזירו שחור.

38 Ye have heard what was said, An
eye for an eye, a tooth for a tooth :
39 but I say unto you, That ye withstand
not evil : [1] but if one would smite
thee on the right cheek, turn unto
40 him the other. And whosoever
wisheth to contend with thee [2] in
judgment, and wisheth to take from
thee thy coat, leave him the cloak
41 also. And he that impresseth thee
for one mile,[3] go with him even twain.
42 And whoso asketh of thee give to him,
and from him that would borrow of
43 thee turn not thou away. Ye have
heard that it was said, Thou shalt
love thy neighbour, and hate thine
44 enemy : but I say unto you, Love
your enemies, do good to them that
hate you, and pray for them which
persecute you and despitefully use
45 you ; [4] in order that ye may become
the children of your Father which is
in heaven : who maketh his sun to
rise on the good and on the evil, and
sendeth rain on the righteous and on
46 the wicked. For if ye love only them

² להריב עמך.   ¹ שלא לעמוד נגד הרע.
³ ואשר יגוש אותך על מיל אחד.
⁴ Cf. Luke 6 : 27, 28.

which love you, what reward have ye ?
do not even transgressors [1] do this ?

47   And if ye ask after the peace of your
brethren only, what do ye exceed ?
48 do not even the Gentiles do this ?   Be
ye therefore perfect, like your Father
which is in heaven who is perfect.

6 1   See that ye bestow not your alms
before men, so that they may see
you : for then ye have no reward on
the part of your Father which is in
2 heaven.   Therefore when thou be-
stowest alms, blow not a trumpet
before thee, like the hypocrites do in
the synagogues and in the streets, in
order that men may honour them.
3 Verily I say unto you, That already
they have received their reward.   But
thou, when thou dispensest alms, thy
left hand shall not know what thy
4 right hand doeth : that thine alms
may be in secret : and thy Father
which seeth in secret shall himself
5 recompense thee in public.[2]   And be
not like the hypocrites when thou
prayest : for they delight to stand in
the assemblies [3] and at the corners of

[3] בגלוי.

[1] בעלי עברה.
[2] במקהלות.

the streets to pray, that men may see them.

Verily I say unto you, That already
6 they have received their reward. But thou, when thou prayest, enter into thine apartment, and shut thy door, and pray to thy Father which is in secret; and thy Father which seeth in secret shall recompense thee in public.

7 And ye, when ye pray, multiply not words [1] like the Gentiles do; who think that in an abundance of
8 words they shall be heard. But be ye not likened unto them : for your Father knoweth what is needful for you, before ye ask him.

9 And ye, thus shall ye pray : Our Father which art in heaven, thy Name
10 be sanctified. Thy kingdom come. Thy will be done, as in heaven so on
11 earth. Give us to-day our continual
12 bread.[2] And forgive us our debts, as
13 we release [3] our debtors. And bring us not into temptation, but deliver us from all evil : for thine is the sovereignty, and the might, and the

---

[1] אל תרבו בדברים.
[2] את לחמנו תמידי תן לנו היום.   מוחלים.

glory, for ever, and for ever and
ever.[1]   Amen.

14 For if ye forgive men their sins,
your Father which is in heaven will
15 also forgive you your sins : but if ye
forgive not men, neither will he for-
16 give you your sins.   And ye, when ye
fast, be not like the hypocrites : for
they begrime and disfigure their faces,[2]
that they may appear in the sight of
men to fast.   Verily I say unto you,
That already they have received their
17 reward.   But thou, when thou fastest,
anoint thine head, and wash thy face ;
18 that thou appear not unto men to
fast, but unto thy Father which is
in secret : who shall recompense thee
19 in public.   Lay not up for yourselves
stores [3] upon earth, where caterpillar
and moth devour,[4] and where thieves
20 break through and steal : but lay up
for yourselves stores in heaven, where
caterpillar and moth waste not, and
21 where thieves do not steal : for just [5]
where your store is, there your heart
22 will be also.   The lamp of thy body is

---

¹ כי לך המלוכה והגבורה וכבוד לעולם ולעולמי עולמים.

² שקודרים ומכהים את פניהם.

³ אוצרות.   ⁴ אשר שם חסיל ועש יאכל.   ⁵ אפו.

thine eye: if therefore thine eye be sound,[1] thy whole body shall be in

23 great light. But if thine eye be bad, thy whole body shall be gloomy.[2] If therefore the light that is in thee be darkness, how great is that darkness!

24 No man can serve two lords: for either he will hate the one, and love the other; or else he will love the one, and hate the other. Ye cannot serve

25 God and mammon. And therefore I say unto you, Be not anxious[3] for your souls, in what ye shall eat, or in what ye shall drink; or for your bodies, wherewith ye shall be clothed. Is not the soul more than food, and

26 the body more than raiment? See the birds of the heavens: for they sow not, neither do they reap, nor gather into their granaries; yet your Father which is in heaven feedeth them. Are ye not much better than

27 they? And which of you by taking thought can add even a single cubit

28 unto his stature? Why, then, are ye anxious about raiment? Consider the lilies of the field, how they grow; yet they toil not, neither do they spin:

³ לא תשתדלו. ² אפל. ¹ תמימות.

29 Of a truth [1] I say unto you, That not even Solomon in all his glory was so arrayed like one of them.

30 Wherefore, if God so clothe the herb of the field, which to-day is, and to-morrow is cast into the oven, how much more so you, O little of faith ?

31 Therefore be not anxious, saying, What shall we eat ? or, What shall we drink ? or, What shall we wear ?

32 (For after all these things do Gentiles seek : [2]) for your Father which is in heaven knoweth that ye have need

33 of all these things. Therefore seek ye at the first the dominion of God,[3] and all his righteousness ; and all these

34 things shall be added unto you. And be not anxious for the morrow : for the morrow's day shall be anxious for itself. Sufficient unto the day is the evil thereof.[4]

7 1 Judge not, and ye shall not be judged : condemn not, and ye shall

2 not be condemned.[5] For with what judgment ye judge, ye shall be

---

¹ אמנם. ² ידרשו.

³ לכן בתחילה בקשו את ממלכת האלהים.

⁴ תשפוק ליום רעתו.

⁵ אל תחייבו ולא תחייבו. (Cf. Luke 6 : 37.)

judged : and with what measure ye mete, it shall be measured to you again.

3 And how seest thou the splinter [1] in thy brother's eye, but seest not the beam [2] that is in thine own eye ?

4 And how sayest thou to thy brother, Suffer it now, brother,[3] that I may pull out the splinter out of thine eye ; and, behold, a beam is in thine own

5 eye ? Thou hypocrite, pull out at the first the beam from thine own eye ; and then thou shalt be able to see to pull out the splinter out of thy

6 brother's eye. Give not a holy thing unto the dogs, neither cast ye pearls before swine, lest they trample them with their feet, and the dogs turn

7 again and rend them.[4] Ask, and it shall be given unto you ; seek, and ye shall find ; knock, and it shall be

8 opened unto you : for every one that asketh receiveth ; and he that seeketh findeth ; and to him that knocketh

9 it shall be opened. And which of you, whose son shall ask of him bread, his

---

[1] קסם.

[2] קורה.

[3] אחי הרף נא·   (Cf. Luke 6 : 42.)

[4] וישובו הכלבים ויסחבום·

father will deliver unto him a stone ? [1]

10 Or, whose son shall ask of him fish,
his father will put into his hand a

11 serpent ?   If ye then, being evil, know
how to seek to give good gifts [2] unto
your children, how much more so
your Father which is in heaven, which
giveth good gifts to them that seek

12 of him and ask him ? [3] Therefore
whatsoever ye would that men should
do to you, do ye even so to them :
for this is the Law and the Prophets.

13 Enter ye in by the narrow gate : for
wide is the gate, and wide the way,
that leadeth to destruction,[4] and many

14 there be which go in thereat : how
narrow is the gate, and narrow the
way, which leadeth unto life, and few

15 there be that find it.   Be warned of
false prophets,[5] which come to you in
sheep's clothing, but beneath their
clothing they are as full of deceit as
ravening wolves.[6]

[1] ומי ביניכם שישאל ממנו בנו את הלחם וימסר לו אביו את
האבן. (Cf. Luke 11 : 11.)
[2] תדעו לכם לבקש לתת מתנות טובות.
[3] שיתן מתנות טובות לכל דורשיו ושואליו.
[4] אל האבדון. (Abaddon.)
[5] הזהרו מנביאי השקר.
[6] והם תוך לבושם מרמה מלאים כזאבים הטורפים.

16 But by their fruits ye shall recognise them. Are grape clusters gathered from thorns, or figs from thistles ? [1]

17 Even so every good tree yieldeth good fruits ; but every bad tree yieldeth

18 bad fruits. A good tree cannot yield bad fruits, neither can a bad tree

19 yield good fruits. But indeed every tree that yieldeth not good fruit is hewn down, and cast into the fire.

20 And ye, by their fruits ye shall know

21 them. Not every one that saith unto me, Lord, lord, shall enter into the kingdom of Heaven ; but he that doeth the will of my Father which is in heaven, the same shall enter with me into the kingdom of Heaven.[2]

22 Many will say unto me in that day, Lord, lord, have we not prophesied in thy name ? and in thy name have cast out demons ? and in thy name

23 done many powerful works ? [3] And then will I profess unto them, that I know them not : [4] Withdraw from

24 me, all ye workers of iniquity.[5] Who-

[1] ומפרותיהם תכירום הילקטו מהקוצים ענבים ומן הדרדרים תאנים

[2] הוא יבא עמי במלכות שמים׃

[3] כחות רבות.   [4] שלא ידעתי אותם.

[5] סורו ממני כל פועלי און. (Ps. 6 : 8 [9].)

soever heareth these my words, and
doeth them, is likened unto a wise
man, which built his house upon the
25 rock : and the rain descended, and
the floods came, and the winds blew,
and beat upon that house ; it fell
not : for it was founded upon the
26 rock. And whosoever heareth these
my words, and doeth them not, is
likened unto a foolish man, which
27 built his house upon the sand : and
the rain descended, and the floods
came, and the winds blew upon it,
and beat upon the house ; it fell :
28 and great was the fall of it. And
it came to pass, that when Jesus had
ended these words, the crowds mar-
29 velled at his teaching : for he was
teaching as one having ability of his
own, and not from the mouth of the
scribes and Pharisees.[1]

8 1 When Jesus was come down from
the mountain, much people followed
2 him. And, behold, there came a leper
and did him homage, saying, If thou
desirest, thou canst make me clean.
3 Then Jesus put forth his hand, and
touched him, and saith, I do desire ;

¹ כי היה ממד כלמו מי שבידו היכולת ולא מפי סופרים ופרושים.

be thou clean. And immediately he
4 was cleansed from his leprosy. And
Jesus saith unto him, See thou tell
no man ; but go thy way, and shew
thyself to the priest, and bring unto
him thine offering, as Moses com-
5 manded them for a testimony.[1] And
when Jesus was entered into Kephar-
Nahum, there drew nigh unto him a
centurion, and entreated him, saying,
6 Lord, my son lieth in the house, and
he is paralytic, and sore afflicted.
7 And Jesus saith unto him, I will come
8 and heal him. But the centurion
answered and said, Lord, I am not
ready [2] that thou shouldest come under
my roof : but only speak a word,
9 and my son shall be healed. For
even I am placed under the authority
of another man, and under me are
valiant men : [3] and if I say to this
one, Go, then he goeth ; and to
another, Come, then he cometh ; and
to my servant, Do this, then he doeth
10 it. Now when Jesus heard, he marvelled, and saith to them that followed

---

[1] והבא אליו קרבנך כאשר צוה משה להם לעדות.
[2] אני לא נכון.
[3] כי גם אני הושמתי תחת ממשלת אדם אחר ותחתי אנשי חיל.

him, Verily I say unto you, I have
not found such faith as this in Israel.[1]

11 And I say unto you, That many
shall come from the east and from
the west, and shall recline [2] with
Abraham, Isaac, and Jacob, in the
12 kingdom of Heaven. But the children of the kingdom shall be cast
into the darkness outside : [3] and
there, shall be weeping and gnash-
13 ing of teeth. And Jesus saith
unto the centurion, Go thy way ;
and as thou hast believed, be it unto
thee.

And the boy was healed the same
14 hour. And when Jesus was come into
Kepha's house, he saw his mother-in-
law lying in a continual burning fever.[4]
15 And he touched her hand, and the
burning fever left her : and she arose
16 and ministered unto them. And when
it was evening, they brought unto him
many that were possessed of demons :
and he, by his word alone, cast out
for them the spirits, and healed them
17 that were in evil case : to establish

[1] לא מצאתי כזה אמונה בישראל.
[2] וירבצו.
[3] ישלחו אל חושך החיצון.
[4] בקדחת תמידי.

what was spoken by Isaiah the prophet, who said, Himself took our
sicknesses, and suffered our pains.[1]
18 Now when Jesus saw great crowds
surrounding him, he commanded his
disciples to go unto the other side of
19 the sea. Then one of the scribes
approached, and saith unto him,
Rabbi, I will follow thee whitherso-
20 ever thou goest. And Jesus saith
unto him, Foxes have holes, and the
birds of the heavens nests ; but the
son of Man hath not a floor whereon
21 he may lay his head.[2] And another
of his disciples said unto him, Give
me leave until I bury my father.[3]
22 But Jesus answered him, Come after
me ; and leave the dead to bury their
23 dead. And he went up into the ship,
and his disciples came after him.
24 And, behold, there was a great storm
at sea, and the ship was covered with
the waves : but he himself was
25 asleep. And his disciples drew nigh

[1] חלײנו הוא ישא ומכאובינו סבלם. (Isa. 53 : 4.)

[2] ולבן אדם אין להם קרקע ששם ישים את ראשו
(note the plural להם).

[3] חנח לי עד שאקבור את אבי.

Jesus, in replying, takes up the disciples' plea, "Give me leave,"
and says, "Leave the dead."

unto him, and awoke him, saying,
26 Lord, save us lest we perish. Then
Jesus saith unto them, Why are ye
fearful, O little of faith ? Then he
arose, and commanded the winds and
the sea ; and there was a great calm.
27 But the men marvelled, and said, Who
is this, that the winds and the sea
28 hearken unto him ? Thereafter Jesus
came unto the other side of the sea,
into the country of the Girgashites,[1]
and there came to meet him two
possessed of demons, coming out of
the tombs, and they were exceeding
fierce,[2] so that on account of them
29 no man could pass that way. And,
behold, they cried out, saying, What
have we to do with thee, Jesus, thou
Son of God ? Why art thou come
hither to afflict us before the set
30 time ? [3] Now near by [4] was a herd
31 of many swine feeding. And the
demons entreated him, saying, If thou
cast us out hence, send us away into
32 the herd of swine. And, behold, the
whole herd went with a rush and with

[1] נרגשיים.   [2] וחם אכזרים מאד.
[3] למה באת הלום קורם הזמן לענות אותנו.
[4] קרוב לשם.

great commotion,[1] and precipitated themselves into the sea, and perished.

33 Then the herdsmen fled, and came into the city, and told all these things, and also concerning those in whom were the demons.

34 And, behold, the whole city came out to meet Jesus : and when they saw him, they entreated him that he would pass out of their coasts.

9 1 And Jesus went up into the ship, and departed from the other side of the sea, and came into his own city.

2 And, behold, they brought to him a man stricken with paralysis, lying on a bed : and when Jesus saw their faith, he said unto the paralytic, Have confidence, my son, for thy

3 sins are forgiven thee. And, behold, the scribes said among themselves,

4 Behold, he is a blasphemer. And when Jesus perceived their thoughts, he saith, Wherefore think ye evil in

5 your hearts ? For whether is easier, to say, Thy sins are forgiven thee ;

6 or to say, Arise, and walk ? But that

1 והנה הלך כל העדר בסער ובסעף גדול

or, " and into a steep cleft," reading סעיף.

6

ye may know that the son of Man [1] hath authority on earth to forgive sins, (then said he to the paralytic), Arise, and take up thy bed, and walk into
7 thine house. And he arose, and
8 walked into his house. But when the crowds saw it thus, they were afraid, and gave honour to God, which had given such power to the Son of Man.[1]
9 And as Jesus departed thence, he saw a certain man, sitting in the custom house ; whose name was Matthew : and he saith unto him, Follow me.
10 And it came to pass, as they sat down to eat in the house, behold, many transgressors and sinners came in and eat with Jesus and his disciples.
11 And the Pharisees seeing, they said unto his disciples, Why eateth your teacher with transgressors and sinners ?
12 But when Jesus heard, he answered, saying, There is no need of a physician to heal the healthy, but to heal them
13 that are sick.[2] Therefore, go ye and learn what is written, I desire loving-

---

[1] יראו ויכבדו האלהים אשר נתן הכח הזה לבן האדם.

N.B.—The term בן אדם signifies the generality of men ("son of Man"), while בן האדם refers to Christ ("Son of Man").

[2] אין צריך רופא לרפות הבריאים אלא לרפות אותם שהם בחולי.

kindness, and not sacrifice : [1] for I
am not come to call the righteous,
14 but the sinners. Then approached
him the disciples of Jochanan, saying,
Why [do we] and the Pharisees fast
15 oft, but thy disciples fast not ? And
Jesus saith unto them, Can the
children of the bridegroom [2] weep,
as long as they have the bridegroom
with them ? but the days will come,
when the bridegroom shall be taken
from them, and then shall they fast.
16 There is no one who would put a patch
of worthless cloth upon an old robe,
for he taketh away its completeness
from the robe, and his rent is made
17 worse than before. [3] Neither do they
put new wine into worn out wine-
skins, [4] for the wine-skins would be
split, and the wine spilled : but new
wine they put into new wine-skins,
18 and both are preserved. And while
he was speaking these words unto
them, behold, a certain ruler drew

[1] חסד חפצתי ולא זבח. ‎(Hos. 6 : 6.)
[2] בני החתן. ‎(The bridegroom's friends.)
[3] ולא יהיה מי שישלח חתיכת בגד הפסול על שמלה ישנה כי ישא
מלואה משמלה ויהיה בדקו רע יותר מקודם.
[4] בנאדות בלים.

nigh, and did him homage, saying,
Lord, my daughter is but lately dead :
but do thou come and lay thy hand
19 upon her, and she shall live. And
Jesus arose, and followed him with
20 his disciples. And, behold, a woman,
which had an issue of blood twelve
years, approached behind him, and
21 touched the fringe of his garment : for
she said within herself, If I touch his
garment only, I shall be delivered.
22 But Jesus turned, and when he saw
her, he saith, Have confidence, my
daughter ; for thy faith hath delivered thee. And the woman was
23 delivered the same hour. And when
Jesus had obtained entry [1] into the
ruler's house, and saw the pipers
and dirge makers of the people,[2]
24 he said, Withdraw : for the girl is
not dead, but sleepeth. And they de-
25 rided him. But when the multitude
was put forth, he obtained entry, and
took her by the hand, and saith,
26 Arise, arise, and the girl arose.[3] And
this report went forth into all that
27 land. And when Jesus passed over

[1] וקשנכנת ישו.   [2] שרי החלילים והמיה העם.

[3] ויאמר קומי קומי ותקם הנערה.   (Cf. Mark 5 : 41.)

from thence, there followed him two
blind men, crying, and saying, Take
28 pity on us, O Son of David. And
when he was come into the house, the
blind men drew nigh unto him : and
Jesus saith unto them, Believe ye that
I am able to do this for you ? And
they say unto him, Yea, of a truth,
29 lord. Then touched he their eyes,
saying, According to your faith be it
30 done unto you. And their eyes were
opened ; and Jesus straitly charged
them, saying, See that no man know
31 this. But they, when they went
forth, published the report of him in
32 all that land. And as they went out,
behold, they brought to him a man
33 dumb, and possessed of a demon. But
when the demon was cast out of him,
he spake, and was no more dumb : [1]
and the crowds marvelled, saying,
34 It was never so seen in Israel. But
the Pharisees said, By the chief of
the demons he casteth out the demons.
35 And Jesus went about all the cities,
teaching in their synagogues, and de-
claring the tidings of the kingdom,
and healing every sickness and every

[1] דבר ולא היה עוד אלם.

36 disease among the people. But when he saw the crowds, he took pity on them, because they were tired and prostrate,[1] as sheep which have no shepherd.

37 Then said he unto his disciples, There is a plenteous harvest, but the
38 labourers are few ; entreat ye therefore the Lord of the harvest, that he will send forth the labourers to reap his harvest.

10 1 And when he had called out his twelve disciples, he gave them authority over unclean spirits, to cast them out, and to heal every sick-
2 ness and disease. Now the names of the twelve envoys are these ; The first, Simeon, who was called Kepha,
3 and Andrew his brother ; Philip, and Bartholomew ; Jacob [the son of] Zabdi, and Jochanan his brother ; Thomas, and Matthew, who was a transgressor ; and Jacob [the son
4 of] Alphæus, and Thaddæus ; Simeon the merchant,[2] and Judah Iscariot, who delivered him up to death.
5 And Jesus sent forth these twelve, and commanded them, saying, Go ye

[2] הכנעני (or Canaanite).   [1] כי הם טרוחים ושוכבים.

not into the way of the Gentiles, and
into the cities of the Samaritans enter
6 ye not : but go ye unto the lost sheep
7 of the house of Israel. Go, and cry,
saying, Turn ye, turn ye, for the
kingdom of Heaven is nigh at hand.
8 Heal the sick, raise the dead, cleanse
the lepers, and cast out the demons :
for nought ye have received, for
9 nought ye shall give.[1] Provide
neither gold, nor silver, nor lesser
10 coin [2] in your girdles. Pack not for
the journey,[3] either two coats, or
sandals, or a staff : for the labourer
11 is worthy of his food. And into
whatsoever city or town ye shall
enter, enquire who in it is honour-
able ; and there abide until ye go
12 forth from thence. And when ye
obtain entry into an house, ask after
its peace, saying, Peace be with this
13 house. And if this house be honour-
able, it will return unto you your
14 peace.[4] But any man who will not
receive you, nor hearken to the sound

[2] ואל המעות.   [1] חינם לקחתם וחנם תתנו.
[3] אל תלקטו בדרך.
[4] ישוב אליכם שלומכם.

That is, " it will respond to your greeting " (or, " your peace
shall return unto you ").

of your words, go forth outside of the
house or city, and shake off even the
15 dust from your feet. Verily I say
unto you, It shall be easier for the
land of Sodom and Gomorrha in the
day of doom,[1] than for that city.
16 Behold, I send you forth as sheep in
the midst of wolves : be ye therefore
subtle as serpents, and simple as doves.
17 Take heed to yourselves of men : lest
they deliver you up to the courts,[2]
and scourge you with whips in the
18 assemblies ; and ye shall be led unto
officers and kings for my sake, for a
testimony to them and the Gentiles.
19 But when they deliver you up, take
no thought how or what ye shall
speak : for it shall be put into your
mouths in that hour what ye shall
20 answer. For it is not ye that shall
speak, but the Spirit of your Father
21 shall speak in you. And the brother
shall deliver up the brother to death,
and the father the child : and the children shall rise up against their parents,
to cause them to be put to death.
22 And all men shall hate you on account
of my name : but he that endureth

² לעדות.   ¹ ביום הדי.

to the end the same shall be saved.
23 But when they persecute you in one
city, flee ye to another : verily I say
unto you, Ye shall not have finished
the cities of Israel, till the Son of Man
24 be come. There is no disciple above
the teacher, nor servant above his
25 lord. But enough for the disciple
that he be as his rabbi, and the
servant as his lord. If they have
called the master of the house Baal-
Zebub, how much more the children
26 of the house ? Fear them not therefore : for there is nothing covered, that
shall not be revealed ; and hid, that
27 shall not be known. What I tell you
in the darkness, that speak ye in the
light : and what ye hear in the ear,
28 that cry ye upon the roofs. And fear
not them which slay the body, but
cannot slay the soul : but fear ye him
which can destroy both soul and
29 body in Gehinnom. Are not two
sparrows sold for the smallest coin ? [1]
and one of them shall not fall on the
30 ground without your Father. But
the very hairs of your head are all
31 numbered. Fear ye not therefore,

[1] תחת טבע קטן.

for ye are better than many sparrows.
32 Whosoever therefore shall confess me
before men, him will I confess also
before my Father which is in heaven.
33 But whosoever shall deny me before
men, him will I also deny before my
34 Father which is in heaven. Think
not that I am come to send peace on
35 earth : I am not come to send peace,
but the sword. For I am come to
separate a man from his father, and
the daughter from her mother, and
the daughter-in-law from her mother-
36 in-law. And a man's enemies shall be
37 the men of his own house.[1] And whoso
loveth his father and mother more
than me is not worthy of me ; and
whoso loveth son or daughter more
than me is not worthy to be with me
38 in the kingdom of Heaven.[2] And
whoso taketh not his cross, and
followeth me, the same is not worthy
39 of me. Whoso findeth his soul shall
lose it : and he that loseth his soul
40 for my sake shall find it. Whoso receiveth you the same receiveth me,
and he that receiveth me the same

[1] ‏ואויבי אש אנשי ביתו.‏ (Mic. 7 : 6.)
[2] ‏איננו ראי להיות עמי במלכות שמים.‏

41 receiveth him that sent me. Whoso
receiveth the prophet in the name of a
prophet,[1] the same receiveth a prophet's reward ; and whoso receiveth
the righteous man in the name of a
righteous man, the same receiveth a
42 righteous man's reward. And he that
giveth to drink unto one of these little
ones, even a single cup of cold water, in
the name of a disciple, verily I say unto
you, he shall in no wise lose his reward.

11 1 And it came to pass, when Jesus
had finished commanding his twelve
disciples, he passed over from thence
to teach and to proclaim [2] in their
2 cities. Now Jochanan when he heard
in the fortress [3] the deeds of the
Messiah, sent two of his disciples,
3 and saith unto him, Art thou he that
is destined to come,[4] or do we await
4 another ? And Jesus answered and
saith unto them, Go ye and tell
Jochanan what ye have heard and
5 seen : the blind see, the lame walk,
the lepers are cleansed, the deaf hear,
and the dead are raised, the poor are

---

[1] That is, as a prophet, righteous man, etc.

[2] ולהכריז (summon, invite).   [3] בית הסוחר.

[4] עתיד לבא.

6 made happy : [1] and happy is he that
7 is not offended in me. And after
these were departed, Jesus began to
speak unto the crowds concerning
8 Jochanan. What went ye out into
the wilderness to see ? Was it a reed [2]
shaken with the wind ? But what
went ye out to see ? Was it a man
clothed in soft raiment ? [3] behold,
they that be clothed in soft raiment
9 are in kings' houses. Only what went
ye out to see ? The prophet ? yea,
I say unto you, he was more than a
10 prophet. For he it is, concerning
whom it was written, Behold, I send
my messenger, which shall prepare
11 the way before me.[4] Verily I say,
Among them that are born of women
there hath not arisen a greater than
Jochanan the immerser : howbeit he
that is least in the kingdom of Heaven
12 is greater than he. Only from the
days of Jochanan the immerser until
now the kingdom of Heaven is con-
stricted, and the forceful despoil

[1] עניים יאשרו.
[2] קנה (possible play on the word קנא, a zealot).
[3] נלבשו בחלקות (metaph. surrounded with flatteries).
[4] הנני שולח מלאכי ופנה דרך לפני. (Mal. 3 : 1.)

13 it.[1]   For all the Prophets and the Law
14 prophesied until Jochanan.   And if ye
will receive it, this is Elijah which
15 cometh.   Whoso hath ears to hear,
16 let him hear.   Whereunto shall I
compare this generation ?   It is compared to boys which sit in the market,
which call unto their companions, and
17 say, We have played merrily unto
you, and ye have not danced ; we
have played dolefully, and ye have
18 not lamented.[2]   For Jochanan came
neither eating nor drinking, and they
say, He is possessed of a demon.
19 The Son of Man came both eating and
drinking, and they say, Behold the
man a glutton and a drunkard, and a
friend of transgressors and sinners.
But wisdom is justified of her children.[3]
20 Then began he to reproach the cities
wherein his many mighty works were
done, because they turned not from
21 their evil deeds : Woe unto thee,
Chorazin !   woe unto thee, Beth-
zaida !   for if the mighty works were

[1] מלכות שמים באונס היא ומכרחין נחלין אותה.
[2] נגננו לכם ולא דלגתם שרנו קינה ולא קוננתם.
[3] Compare *The Wisdom of Ben Sira* (Heb.), " Wisdom
teacheth her children."

done in Tyre and Zidon, which were
done in you, they would have turned
from evil long ago in sackcloth and
ashes.

22 Surely I say unto you, That it shall
be easier for Tyre and Zidon in the
day of judgment, than for you.

23 And thou, Kephar-Nahum, art thou
not exalted to the heavens? to
Gehinnom shalt thou be brought
down : [1] for if the mighty works were
done in Sodom, which were done
in thee, perhaps [2] it would have re-

24 mained until this day. Of a truth [3]
I say unto you, that it shall be easier
for the land of Sodom in the day of

25 doom, than for thee. At that time
Jesus answered and saith, I give
thanks unto thee, O Father, Lord of
heaven and earth, which hast concealed [4] these things from the wise and
prudent, and hast revealed them unto

26 the lightly esteemed.[5] Yea, O Father :

27 for so was thy will before thee. All
hath been given me of my Father :
and no man knoweth a son, but a
father ; neither knoweth any one the

¹ הלא עד השמים תרומי עד גיהינם תרדי.

⁵ לצעירים ⁴ שהסתרת. ³ אמנם. ² אולי.

Father save a son, and to whomsoever
28 a son willeth to reveal him. Come
unto me, all ye that labour and are
heavy leaden, and I will satisfy you.[1]
29 Take my yoke upon you, and learn of
me; for I am driven out and downcast in spirit:[2] and ye shall find rest
30 for your souls.[3] For my yoke is
gentle, and my burden easy.

12 1 At that time Jesus went through
the grain[4] on the Sabbath; and his
disciples were an hungred, and began
to pluck the ears from the stalks,[5]
2 and to eat. But the Pharisees seeing,
said, Behold, thy disciples do that
which is not right to do on the Sabbath.
3 But he said unto them, Have ye not
read what David did, when he was an
hungred, both he and they that were
4 with him; for he entered into the
house of God, and did eat the shew-
bread, which was not lawful for him
to eat them, neither for them which
were with him, but only for the
5 priests? Have ye not read in the
Law, that the priests profane the

¹ אשביעכם. ² כי נער אני ושפל רוח.
³ ותמצאו מרגוע לנפשותיכם. (Jer. 6 : 16.)
⁴ על זרע. ⁵ ויחלו לקטף שבלים מן הקמות.

Sabbath in the Temple, and are
6 blameless ? But I say unto you,
That here is greater than the Temple.
7 But if ye had known what it meaneth,
I desire loving-kindness, and not sacrifice, ye would not have condemned the
8 guiltless. For the Son of Man is lord
9 even of the Sabbath. And when he
had passed over from thence, he
10 entered into their synagogue : And
behold, a man which had his hand
withered. And they asked him, saying, Is it lawful on the Sabbath to
heal the sick ? [1] And all this was
that they might accuse him before the
11 court of justice.[2] And he said unto
them, What man among you, having
one sheep that shall fall into a pit on
the Sabbath, will not lay hold on it,
12 and lift it out ? And is not a man
better than the sheep ? Wherefore
it is lawful to do well on the Sabbath.
13 Then saith he to the man, Stretch
forth thine hand. And he stretched
it forth ; and it was restored to health,
14 like as the other. Then the Pharisees
went out, and took counsel against
him, how they might destroy him.

² וכל זה כדי להלשינו לבית דין.   ¹ לרפא לחולים.

15 But when Jesus knew, he withdrew
from thence : and many followed him,
16 and he healed them all ; and commanded them that they should not
17 make him known : [1] in order that it
might be established which was spoken
by Isaiah the prophet, who said,
18 Behold my servant, whom I uphold ;
my chosen in whom I am well pleased ;
I have put my Spirit upon him : he
shall bring forth judgment to the
19 Gentiles. He shall not cry, nor lift
up, nor cause his voice to be heard in
20 the street. A bruised reed shall he
not break, and the smoking flax shall
he not quench : he shall bring forth
21 judgment unto truth. He shall not
fail nor be discouraged, till he have set
judgment in the earth : and the isles
22 shall wait for his law.[2] Then was
brought unto him one possessed of a
demon, blind and dumb : and he
healed him, so that he was able both to
23 speak and to see.[3] And all the crowds

[1] שלא יפרסמוהו.

[2] הן עבדי אתמך בו בחירי רצתה נפשי נתתי רוחי עליו משפט
כגוים יוציא לא יצעק ולא ישא ולא ישמיע בחוץ קולו קנה רצוץ לא
יטבור ופשתה כהה לא יכבנה לאמת יוציא משפט לא יכהה ולא
ירוץ עד ישים בארץ משפט ולתורתו איים ייחלו. (Isa. 42 : 1–4.

[3] כדי שיכול לדבר ולראות.

7

marvelled, and said, Is he not the
24 Son of David ?   But when the Pharisees heard, they said, He doth not
cast out the demons, but by Baal-
25 Zebub the chief of the demons.   And
when Jesus knew their thoughts, he
said unto them, Every kingdom
divided against itself is brought to
desolation ; and every city or house
divided against itself shall not stand :
26 and if Satan cast out Satan, he is
divided against himself ; and how then
shall his kingdom stand ?
27   And if I by Baal-Zebub cast out the
demons, by whom do your children
cast out ? therefore they shall be
28 your judges.   But because I am casting out the demons by the Spirit of
God, then the kingdom of God is come
29 unto you.   And how can a man enter
into the strong man's house to plunder
his goods, except he first bind the
strong man ? and then he will plunder
30 his house.   Whoso is not with me the
same is against me ; and whoso
gathereth not with me the same
31 scattereth.   And therefore I say unto
you, Every sin and blasphemy shall
be forgiven man : but the blasphemy

which is against the spirit shall not
32 be forgiven. And every man that
saith a word against the son of Man,
it shall be forgiven him : but he that
saith a word against the Holy Spirit,
it shall not be forgiven him, neither
in this world, nor in the world to come.
33 Either make the tree good, and its
fruit good ; or make the tree bad,
and its fruit bad : for the tree is
34 known from its fruit. Generation of
vipers, how can ye speak good things,
being yourselves evil ? for out of the
abundance of the heart the mouth
35 speaketh. The good man bringeth
forth good things out of his good
store : but the evil man bringeth
forth evil things out of his evil store.
36 And I say unto you, That every
idle word that men shall speak, they
shall render an account thereof [1] in
37 the day of judgment. For by thy
words thou shalt be justified, and by
thy words thou shalt be condemned.
38 Then certain of the scribes and of
the Pharisees answered him, saying,
Rabbenu, we wish to see a sign from
39 thee. But he answered and said unto

י ישיבו עליו טעם.

them, An evil and adulterous generation seeketh a sign ; but no sign shall
be given it except the sign of Jonah

40 the prophet : for as Jonah was three
days and three nights in the fish's
belly, so shall the Son of Man be three
days and three nights in the heart of

41 the earth. And the men of Nineveh
shall arise in the judgment with this
generation, and shall condemn it : [1]
because they repented at the preaching of Jonah ; and, behold, a greater
than Jonah is here.[2]

42 The queen of the south shall arise
in the judgment with this generation,
and shall condemn it : for she came
from the uttermost parts of the earth [3]
to hear the wisdom of Solomon ; and,
behold, a greater than Solomon is

43 here. When the unclean spirit is gone
out of a man, it goeth through dry
places, seeking rest, but findeth none.

44 Then it saith, I will return unto my
house from whence I came out ; and
it cometh, and findeth it empty, and
cleaned out with shovels,[4] and adorned.

45 Then it goeth, and taketh seven other

² והנה יותר מיונה פה.   (cf. Ex. 22 : 9 [8]).   ¹ ויישיעוהו.

⁴ ומטוהר ביעים.   ³ מקצות הארץ.

spirits more wicked than itself, and
they enter in and dwell there : so
that the latter end of that man is
worse than the beginning.[1] Even so
shall it be unto this wicked genera-
46 tion. And as he continued to speak
to the crowds, behold, his mother and
his brethren stood without, and sought
47 to speak with him. Then one saith
unto him, Behold, thy mother and thy
brethren stand without, and are seek-
48 ing thee. But he answered him that
told him, and saith, Which is my
mother ? [2] and who are my brethren ?
49 And he stretched forth his hand toward his disciples, and saith, Behold,
50 my mother and my brethren ! Every
man that doeth the will of my Father
which is in heaven, they are my
brethren, my sisters and my mother.
13 1   The same day Jesus went out of the
2 house, and sat by the sea side. And
great crowds thronged [3] unto him, so
that he went up into the ship, and sat ;
and all the people stood on the sea
3 shore. And he spake much unto them

ותהינה אחריות האדם ההוא רעות מן הראשיות [1]
(cf. Num. 24 : 20 ; Job 42 : 12).

‎[3] ויקבצו.   ‎[2] איזו אמי.

in parables, and saith, Behold, the
4 sower went forth to sow his seed ; and
as he sowed, some of them fell by the
way side, and the birds of the heavens
5 came and ate them up. And others
fell upon the rock,[1] where there was
not much earth : and forthwith they
sprouted, because they had no depth
6 in the earth : and when the sun was
risen, they were dried up ; and because
they had no root, they withered away.
7 And others fell among the thorns ;
and the thorns grew up, and choked
8 them. But others fell into good
ground, and brought forth fruit, one
an hundredfold, and another sixty,
9 and another thirtyfold. Whoso
hath ears to hear, let him hear.
10 And his disciples drew nigh unto him,
and said unto him, Lord, why speakest
11 thou with us in parables ? [2] And he

---

[1] עַל הַסֶּלַע.

[2] אדני למה תדבר עמנו במשלים

(vv. 10–13). Jesus is speaking equally to the disciples in
parables, because of spies and informers in the crowd, but to
them he privately explains all things. " I am speaking to you
(the disciples and loyal people) in parables, that they (the
informers and disloyal people) seeing shall not see," etc. Jesus
used a necessary precaution. Here and elsewhere in the Gospel
the words " whoso hath ears to hear, let him hear," are a
warning to look out for a hidden meaning in the speech.

answered and saith unto them, Because it is given unto you to understand the secrets of the kingdom of
Heaven, but to these it is not given.
12 For whoso hath, to him shall be given,
and he shall abound : but whoso
hath not, even what he hath shall
13 be taken from him. And therefore I
am speaking to you in parables ; that
they seeing shall not see ; and hearing
shall not hear, neither shall they
14 understand. To establish in them the
prophecy of Isaiah, he who said, Hearing, hear ye, but understand not ; and
15 seeing, see ye, but perceive not : stul-
tify this people's heart, and dull its
ears, and glue up its eyes ; lest it
see with its eyes, and hear with its
ears, and understand with its heart,
16 and return, and be healed.[1] But
happy are your eyes, for they see :
and your ears, for they hear.
17 Verily I say unto you, That many
prophets and righteous men have
desired to see what ye are seeing, but
have not seen ; and to hear what ye

[1] שמעו שמוע ואל תבינו וראו ראו ואל תדעו השמן לב העם הזה
ואזניו הכבד ועיניו השע פן יראה בעיניו ובאזניו ישמע ולבבו יבין
ושב ורפא לו. (Isa. 6 : 9, 10.)

are hearing, but have not heard.
18 Hear ye therefore the parable of the
19 sower. Whosoever heareth the word
of the kingdom, and understandeth
not, the evil one cometh, and plucketh
out that which was sown in his heart.
And this is that which was sown by
20 the way side. But as for that which
was sown on the rock, this is he that
heareth the word, and straightway [1]
21 with joy receiveth it ; but is like unto
the seed which hath no root,[2] for he
endureth but for an hour : and when
tribulation or persecution ariseth,[3] he
is immediately offended.

22   And as for that which was sown
among the thorns, the same is he that
heareth the word of God,[4] but the
care of this world, and the lust for
the false mammon,[5] choke the word,
23 and he becometh unfruitful. But as
for that which was sown on good
ground, the same is he that heareth
the word, and understandeth, and
bringeth forth fruit ; and one pro-
duceth an hundredfold, and another

---

[2] ‏ודומה לזרע שאין לה שורש.‏   [1] ‏ופתאום.‏

[3] Omitting " because of the word."

[5] ‏ותאות שקר הממון.‏   [4] ‏דבר האלהים.‏

24 sixty, and another thirtyfold. Yet
another parable put he forth unto
them, saying, The kingdom of Heaven
is like unto a man which sowed good

25 seed in his field : but while men slept,
his enemy came and sowed nettles
among the wheat, and went his way.

26 But when the blade grew up, and produced the fruit, then appeared there

27 the nettles also. So the servants of
the householder drew nigh and said
unto him, Lord, didst not thou sow
good seed in thy field ? from whence
then came the nettles into it ?

28   And he saith unto them, A man that
is an enemy hath done this.[1] Then the
servants said unto him, Wilt thou
that we go and gather them up ?

29 But he saith, Nay ; lest while ye
gather up the nettles, ye root up also

30 the wheat with them. Let both grow
together until the harvest : and at
harvest time I will say to the reapers,
Gather first the nettles, and bind
them in bundles for burning : but
gather the wheat into my floor.

31   Yet another parable put he forth
unto them, saying, The kingdom of

¹ אדם אויב עשה זאת.

Heaven is likened unto a grain of mustard seed, which a man took and
32 sowed it in his field : which indeed is the least of all seeds : but when it is grown, becometh the greatest of herbs, and becometh a tree, so that the birds of the heavens come and nest in the branches thereof.

33 Again he spake unto them another parable ; The kingdom of Heaven is likened unto leaven, which a woman took and hid in three measures of meal, till the whole should be leavened.

34 All these are the sayings of Jesus in parables unto the crowds ; [1] and without parables spake he not with them :
35 to fulfil the utterance of the prophet who said, I will open my mouth in a parable : I will utter dark sayings of old.[2]

36 Then he sent the crowds away, and entered into the house : and his disciples approached him, saying, Explain unto us the parable of the nettles
37 of the field. Then he answered and saith, He that sowed the good seed is
38 the Son of Man ; and the field is the world ; and the good seed they are

[1] כל אלה דברי ישו במשלים אל הכיתות.
[2] אפתחה במשל פי אביעה חידות מני קדם. (Ps. 78 : 2.)

the children of the kingdom ; but
the nettles they are the children of
39 Belial ; and the enemy that sowed
them is Satan ; and the harvest is
the end of the world ; and the reapers
40 they are the angels. And just as the
nettles were gathered up and burned
in the fire ; so shall it be in the end
41 of the world. For the Son of Man
shall send forth his angels, and they
shall gather out of his kingdom all
offences, and them which do iniquity ; [1]
42 and shall cast them into the furnace
of fire : there, shall be weeping and
43 gnashing of teeth. Then shall the
righteous shine forth as the sun in the
kingdom of their Father. Whoso hath
44 ears to hear, let him hear. The
kingdom of Heaven is likened unto
treasure hid in a field ; which if a man
find, he hideth, and out of his joy he
goeth and selleth all that he hath, and
45 buyeth that field. Again, the kingdom of Heaven is likened unto a man
that is a merchant, seeking goodly
46 pearls : who, when he had found one
precious pearl, went and sold all that
he had, and bought it.

[1] ואתם שעשו פשע.

47   Again, the kingdom of Heaven is
likened unto a drag net,[1] that was
cast into the sea, and gathered of
48 every kind of fish : which, they,
drawing forth when it was full, and
sitting down on the sea shore, chose
the good and put them into vessels,
49 but the bad they cast away. So
shall it be in the end of the world : for
the angels shall go forth, and separate
the wicked from among the righteous,
50 and shall cast them into the furnace
of fire : there, shall be weeping and
51 gnashing of teeth.   [2] Have ye understood all these things ?   And they say
unto him, Yea.

52   Then saith he unto them, Therefore
every scribe taught in the kingdom of
Heaven is like unto a man that is an
householder, which bringeth forth out
53 of his store new and old. And it
came to pass, when Jesus had finished
speaking these parables, he passed
54 over from thence.   And when he was
come into his native land,[3] he taught
them in their synagogues, and they
marvelled, saying, Whence hath he

---

[2] Omitting " Jesus saith unto them."   .למכמורת [1]

.ארץ מולדתו [3]

55 this wisdom, and might ? Is he not
the smith's son ? [1] Is not his mother
called Miriam, and his brethren, Jacob,
and Joseph, and Simeon, and Judah ?
56 And are not his sisters all with us ?
Whence then hath he all these things ?
57 And they were offended in him.

But Jesus saith unto them, There is
no prophet without honour, except in
his native place, and in his own house.
58 And he did not many mighty works
there because of their stubbornness.[2]

14 1 At that time Herod the tetrarch [3]
heard the report concerning Jesus,
2 and saith unto his young men, This
is Jochanan the immerser ; he is risen
from the dead ; and therefore the
powers are working in him.[4]
3 For Herod had laid hold on
Jochanan, and bound him, and put
him in prison from before Herodias,
4 his brother's [5] wife. For she said
unto him, Jochanan is not worthy to
5 be with thee.[6] And he wished to slay

---

² בעבור סררותם.   ¹ הלא זה בן נפחא.

⁴ ועל כן הכחות יפעלו בו.   ³ אחד מארבעה נשיאים.

⁵ Omitting " Philip " with Vulg. D. etc. The brother's
name was Herod, not Philip. Cf. Josephus XVIII. v. 1.

⁶ כי אמרה אליו יוחנן אינו ראוי שיהיה עמך.

him, but he feared the people ; for
he was as a prophet in their eyes.

6   Now on Herod's birthday, the
daughter of Herodias danced in the
midst, and she won approval in the
7 eyes of Herod.   And he swore unto
her with an oath to give her whatso-
8 ever she should ask of him.   And she,
being instructed of her mother, saith,
Give me here in a dish the head of
Jochanan the immerser.

9   And it grieved the king : but on
account of the oath, and on account
of them which sat together with him
at the table, he commanded it to be
10 given her.   And he sent, and cut off
the head of Jochanan which was in
11 the fortress ; that his head might be
brought in a dish, and that they might
give it to the girl.   And they did so.[1]
And it was given to the girl, and she
12 brought it to her mother.   Then his
disciples approached, and removed his
body, and buried it, and his disciples
13 came and told Jesus.   And when he
heard it, he escaped from thence into
a desert place alone.

Now when the crowds heard, they

¹ ויתנו אותו לנערה ויעשו כן.

followed him on foot out of their
14 cities. And he went forth, and saw
much people, and took pity on them,
15 and healed their sick. And when evening was come, his disciples drew nigh
unto him, saying, The place is desolate,
and the hour is already past ; take
leave of the crowds, therefore, that
they may go into the villages, and
16 buy themselves food. But Jesus saith
unto them, There is no need for them
17 to go ; give ye them to eat. And
they answered him, We have here but
18 five loaves, and two fishes. And he
saith unto them, Bring them hither
19 to me. And he commanded the people
to sit down to eat on the grass in the
field,[1] and he took the five loaves, and
the two fishes, and lifting up his eyes
to heaven, he blessed, and brake, and
gave the loaves to his disciples, and
20 his disciples gave to the crowds. And
they did all eat, and were satisfied :
and there were left over [2] unto them
twelve baskets full of the fragments.
21 And the number of them that did eat
was five thousand men, beside the
22 women and infants. And immedi-

[2] ונשארו.   [1] על החציר בשדה.

ately Jesus urged his disciples to go up into a ship, and to go before him across the sea, while he took leave of
23 the crowds. And when he had taken leave of the people, he went up alone into the mountain to pray : and it was evening, and he was there alone.
24 Now the ship was tossed in the midst of the sea by the waves : for the wind
25 was contrary to them. And it came to pass in the fourth watch of the night that he came unto them, and
26 walked by the sea.[1] And when they saw him walking by the sea, they were terrified, and said, It is a malignant spirit ; [2] and they cried out for fear.
27 But straightway Jesus spake unto them, saying, Have confidence ; for it is I ; be not afraid.
28   Then Kepha answered and saith, Lord, if it be thou, bid me come unto
29 thee over the water.[3] And he said, Come. So Kepha descended from the ship, and went over the water, to
30 come to Jesus. But when he saw the wind boisterous, he was exceed- ingly afraid lest he should sink, and

[2] כי מזיק הוא.   or "on the sea."   על הים [1]
                          or "on the water."   על המים [3]

31 cried out, saying, Lord, save me. And immediately Jesus stretched forth his hand, and caught him, and saith unto him, O thou little in faith, wherefore
32 didst thou doubt ? And when they were gone up into the ship, immedi-
33 ately the wind subsided. And when they were in the ship, they came and did him homage, saying, In truth
34 thou art the Son of God. And they departed from over the sea, and came
35 into the land of Ge-nossar.[1] And the men of that place, when they knew it, sent into all that land, and brought unto him all that were in evil
36 case ; and entreated him that they might touch the fringe of his garment : and as many as touched were delivered.

15 1 Then drew nigh unto him scribes and Pharisees from Jerusalem, saying,
2 Why do thy disciples transgress the decrees of the elders ?[2] for they cleanse not their hands when they eat bread.
3 But he answered them and saith, And why do ye transgress the commandments of God by means of your de-

---

[1] גינוסר   (perhaps "the valley of timber").
[2] גזירות הזקנים.

8

4 crees ? Is it not written in your Law [1]
from the mouth of God, Honour thy
father and thy mother ? [2] And moreover written, And he that curseth his
father and his mother shall surely
5 die ? [3] But ye say, Whosoever saith
unto father and mother, It is all a
gift, whatsoever of mine might profit
6 thee ; [4] and he honoureth not his
father and his mother. Thus have ye
made void the commandments of God
on account of your decrees.

7 Ye hypocrites, Isaiah did well indeed
to prophesy concerning you, saying,
8 This people honoureth me with its
mouth and lips, but its heart is far
9 from me, and their fear toward me
is become a taught commandment
10 of men.[5] Then he called the crowds
to himself, and saith, Hear, and
11 know : Whatso entereth into the
mouth defileth not the man ; but what
proceedeth out of the mouth, that
12 defileth the man. Then his disciples

¹ הלא כתוב בתורתכם.
² כבד את אביך ואת אמך. (Ex. 20 : 12.)
³ ומקלל אביו ואמו מות יומת. (Ex. 21 : 17.)
⁴ כל מתן שהוא ממני היא תועלתך.
⁵ העם הזה בפיו ובשפתיו כבדוני ולבו רחק ממני ותהי יראתם אותי
מצות אנשים מלומדה. (Isa. 29 : 13.)

approached him, and said, Know thou
that the Pharisees which heard this
13 saying were annoyed.[1]   But Jesus
answered and saith, Every plant,
which my Father which is in heaven
hath not planted, shall be rooted up.
14 Leave them alone : for they be blind,
and leaders of the blind.   And if the
blind lead another blind, both of them
shall fall into the ditch.
15   Then answered Kepha and saith unto
him, Explain unto us this parable.
16 And Jesus saith, Are ye also yet
17 without understanding ?   Do ye not
understand, that whatsoever entereth
into the mouth entereth into the
belly, and is cast out in the draught ?
18 But those things which proceed out
of the mouth, they proceed from the
heart ;   and they are those things
19 which defile the man.   For from the
heart proceed evil thoughts, murders,
adulteries, fornications, thefts, false
20 witness, and blasphemies : these are
those things which defile the man :
but that a man should eat without
washing his hands that defileth not
21 the man.   Then Jesus went forth

[1] נכעסו.

from thence, and entered into the
22 parts of Tyre and Zidon. And, behold, a merchant woman [1] came forth
out of those coasts, and cried out, and
said unto him, Take pity on me, O
Lord, thou Son of David ; for my
daughter is sore afflicted of a demon. [2]
23 But Jesus answered her not at all.
And his disciples drew nigh and
entreated him, saying, Send her
24 away ; for she crieth after us. But
he answered and saith, I was not sent
but unto the lost sheep of the house
25 of Israel. Then came she and pros-
trated herself to the ground unto him,
26 and saith, Lord, deliver me. But
Jesus answered and saith, It is not
good to take the children's bread,
27 and to give it to the dogs. Then
answered she and said, Truth certainly, Lord : [3] but the dogs even they
eat of the fragments which fall under
28 their masters' table. Then Jesus
answered and saith unto her, O

[1] אשה כנענית
(lit, a Canaanite woman). We should possibly render this with
Justin Martyr—a Phœnician woman ; the Hebrew may mean
either.
[2] Cf. 2 Kings 6 : 26.

[3] אמת כן אדני.

woman, how great is thy faith : be
it unto thee even as it is in thine
heart. And her daughter was healed
the same hour.

29 And Jesus passed over from thence,
and came by the sea of Galilee ;
and went up into a mountain, and
30 sat down there. And there drew
nigh unto him great crowds, having
with them dumb, blind, lame,
maimed,[1] and many others, and laid
them down at his feet ; and he healed
31 them. And the people marvelled,
when they saw the dumb speaking,
and the lame walking, and the blind
seeing : and they magnified the God
32 of Israel. Then Jesus called his
disciples, and saith unto them, I have
compassion for the people, because
it is now three days that they abide
with me in the wilderness, and they
have nothing that they may eat : and
I will not let them go fasting, lest they
faint by the way.

33 And his disciples say unto him,
Whence should we have bread enough
in the wilderness, to satisfy this
34 people ? And Jesus saith unto them,

‎¹ חלשים.

How many cakes of bread [1] have ye ?
And they answered and said, Seven,
35 and a few small fishes. Then he
commanded the people to sit down on
36 the ground. And he took the seven
cakes of bread and the fishes, and
gave thanks, and brake, and gave to
his disciples, and they gave to the
37 people. And they did all eat, and
were satisfied : and of what was left
over by the crowds they took up
38 seven baskets full. And they that
did eat were four thousand men,
39 beside the infants and women. And
he took leave of the crowds, and went
up into the ship, and came into the
coast of Magdala.

16 1 And there approached him Pharisees
and Zadducees tempting and asking
him that he would shew a single sign
2 from Heaven. But he answered them,
and saith unto them, When it is
evening, ye say, It is destined to be
fine by the heavens : for the heavens
3 are ruddy. And at daybreak, It will
be stormy : for the heavens are
lowring in their ruddiness.

And,[2] behold, ye know how to

---

[2] Omitting " ye hypocrites."   .כברי לחם [1]

judge the face of the heavens ; but ye cannot discern the signs of the times. 4 An evil and lewd stock [1] seeketh a sign ; and no sign shall be given it, but the sign of Jonah the prophet.

And he left them, and went his 5 way. And when his disciples were come to the other side of the sea, they had 6 forgotten to take bread. And he said unto them, See and beware of the leaven [2] of the Pharisees and Zad-7 ducees. And they reasoned among themselves, saying, Is it because we 8 have taken no bread ? And when Jesus knew, he saith, What are ye thinking, O little of faith, that it is because ye have taken no bread ? 9 Do ye not yet understand, neither remember the five loaves to the five thousand men, and how many 10 baskets ye took up ? Neither the seven loaves to the four thousand men, and how many baskets ye took 11 up ? And why then do ye not under-stand that it was not concerning loaves that I spake to you, Beware of the leaven of the Pharisees and

---

[1] יהום רע וזימה.

[2] ממחמצת. (*i.e.* leavened food. Cf. Ex. 12 : 19.)

12 Zadducees ? Then they heard and
understood that he said not to beware of the leaven of bread, but of
the doctrine of the Pharisees and
13 Zadducees. And Jesus came into the
coasts of Cæsarea Philippi. And he
asked one and all [1] of his disciples,
saying, Whom do the children of men
14 say that the Son of Man is ? And they
say, Some, that he is Jochanan the
immerser : and some, Elijah ; and
others, Jeremiah, or another of the
prophets.

15   And Jesus saith unto them, And
ye, whom say ye that I am ?
16   Then answered Simeon Kepha, saying, Thou art Messiah, the Son of the
17 living God. And Jesus answered and
saith unto him, Happy art thou,
Simeon the son of Jonah : for this
was not revealed unto flesh and blood,
but unto thee, when it was revealed
unto thee by my Father which is in
18 heaven.[2] And I say unto thee, That
thou art Kepha, and upon this rock [3]

---

[1] לכל לאחד.

[2] אשריך שמעון בן יונה כי לבשר ודם לא נגלה זה כי אם לד
שנגלה לך מאבי שהוא בשמים.

[3] ועל הכיפה הזאת.

I will build my assembly ; and the gates of the nether world shall not
19 prevail against thee.[1]   And unto thee will I give the keys of the kingdom of Heaven : and whatsoever thou shalt bind on earth shall be bound in Heaven : and whatsoever thou shalt loose on earth shall be loosed in heaven.

20 Then commanded he his disciples that they should tell no man that he,
21 Jesus, was the Messiah. And then began Jesus to make known to his disciples, that he needs must go to Jerusalem, and to suffer there many scourgings, and many mockings,[2] of the elders and scribes, and of the chief priests, and to be slain, and to rise
22 again the third day. Then Kepha took him, and began to rebuke him, saying, Far be it from thee, Lord :
23 all this shall not be unto thee. But he turned, and saith unto Kepha, Follow me, satan : [3] thou art an offence unto me : for thou savourest not the things that be of God, but

[1] וְשַׁעֲרֵי תַחְתִּיּוֹת לֹא יִגְבְּרוּ עָלֶיךָ.
[2] יִסּוּרִים רַבִּים וְגִידוּפִים רַבִּים.
[3] לֵךְ אַחֲרַי שָׂטָן.   (*i.e.* Follow me, adversary.)

24 those that be of men. Then said
Jesus unto his disciples, Whoso willeth
to follow me, let him reject himself,[1]
and take up his cross, and follow me.

25   For whoso shall desire to save his
soul shall lose it : and whoso shall lose
his soul for my sake, the same shall find
26 it.   For what shall it profit a man, if
he gain the whole world, and in his
own soul receive injury ? [2] or what
exchange shall a man give for his
27 soul ? [3] For the Son of Man shall
come in the glory of his Father with
his angels ;   and then shall he pay
every man, each according to his
28 deeds.   Verily I say unto you, There
be those standing here, which shall
not taste death, till they see the Son
of Man's kingdom that cometh.[4]

17 1 And after six days Jesus took
Kepha, and Jacob, and Jochanan his
brother, and bringeth them up into an
2 high mountain apart, and the fashion
of his face was altered before them : [5]
and his face did shine as the sun, and

[1] ימאס את עצמו.   [2] ובנפשו נזק ישא.
[3] או איזו תמורה יתן האדם תחת נפשו.
[4] עד שיראו בן האדם הבאה מלכותו.
[5] ויצטיירו פניו לפניהם.

his raiment became white as the snow.[1]

3 And, behold, there appeared unto them Moses and Elijah talking with
4 him.   Then answered Kepha, and saith unto Jesus, Lord, it is good for us to be here : if thou wilt, let us make here three tabernacles ; for thee one, for Moses one, and for Elijah
5 one. While yet speaking, behold, a bright cloud overshadowed them.

And, behold, a voice out of the cloud said, This is my beloved Son, with whom I am well pleased ; hear
6 ye him.[2] And when the disciples heard, they fell on their faces, and were
7 sore afraid. But Jesus approached and touched them, and saith unto them, Arise, and be not afraid.
8 And when they had lifted up their eyes, they saw no one, save Jesus only.
9   And as they came down from the mountain, Jesus commanded them, saying, Tell no man the vision which ye have seen,[3] until the Son of Man be risen from the dead.
10   And the disciples asked him, saying,

[1] כמו שלג. (Cf. Mark 9 : 3.)
[2] הזה הוא בני אהובי אשר רציתי אותו שמעו.
[3] אשר ראיתם. (Cf. Mark 9 : 9.)

Why then say the scribes that Elijah
11 needs must come first? And he
answered and saith unto them, Elijah
shall surely come, and restore all
12 things. And I say unto you, That
Elijah is come already, and they knew
him not, but have done unto him
whatsoever they chose. Likewise
shall the Son of Man receive and bear
13 scourgings from them.[1] Then the
disciples heard and understood that
he was speaking of the immerser
Jochanan, when he spake unto them.
14 And when they were come to the
crowd, there drew nigh unto him a
certain man, and fell on his knees
15 before him, saying, Lord, have compassion on my son: for he is epileptic,
and with this sickness he is sore
afflicted :[2] for ofttimes he falleth
into the fire, and ofttimes he falleth
16 into the water. And I brought him
to thy disciples, but they could not
17 cure him. Then Jesus answered and
saith, O stubborn and perverse generation, how long shall I be with you?
how long shall I suffer you? bring

[1] וכן בן האדם יקבל וישא יסורים מהם.
[2] ומאותו החולי הוא מענה מאד.

18 him to me.   And Jesus rebuked him ;
   and the demon went out of him : and
   the boy was cured the same hour.

19   Then drew nigh unto him the disciples privily, and asked him, Why
20 could not we cast him out ?   And he
   answered them and saith, On account
   of your lack of faith.   Verily I say
   unto you, If ye have faith as a grain of
   mustard seed, and shall say unto this
   mountain, Pass away hence ; it will
   immediately   pass   away ;   and   the
   thing shall not be withheld from you.[1]
21 But this kind is not cast out but by
22 prayer and fasting.   And as they were
   going into Galilee, Jesus spake unto
   them and saith, The Son of Man shall
   be betrayed into the hands of men :
23 and they shall slay him, and the third
   day he shall rise again.   And they
24 were   sore   grieved.   And when they
   were come into Kephar-Nahum, they
   that received the drachma [2] drew nigh
   unto Kepha, and said unto him, Doth
25 your teacher pay the drachma ?   And
   he saith, Certainly.   And as he came
   into the house, Jesus prevented him,
   saying, How   seemeth   it   to   thee,

(Gr. δραχμή.)   ² דרכמון.   ¹ ולא ימנע אותו הדבר מכם.

Simeon ? The kings of the earth, of whom do they receive tribute and custom ? [1] of their own children, or of
26 strangers ? And he said, Of strangers. Then Jesus saith unto him, If so, the
27 children are free. But in order that we may not provoke them, go thou to the sea, and cast the baited net,[2] and take the fish that first cometh up ; and when thou hast opened its mouth, thou shalt find a litra : [3] that take, and give unto them for me and thee.

18 1 The same hour the disciples drew nigh unto Jesus, saying, Who shall be greatest in the kingdom of Heaven ?
2 And Jesus called a certain boy, and stood him in the midst of them,
3 and saith, Verily I say unto you, Unless ye repent, and become as children, ye shall not enter into the
4 kingdom of Heaven. Whosoever therefore shall humble himself as this boy, the same shall be greatest in the
5 kingdom of Heaven. And whoso receiveth one such boy as this in
6 my name receiveth me. And whoso offendeth one of these little ones which

(Gr. λίτρα.) לטר. [3]   מצודה. [2]   מס ותרומה. [1]

believe in me, it were better for him
that an upper millstone [1] were hanged
about his neck, and that he were cast
7 into the depth of the sea. Woe unto
the world because of offences ! It
must needs be that offences come ;
but woe to that man by whom the
offence cometh !

8   And if thy hand or thy foot offend
thee, cut it off, and cast it from thee :
for it is better for thee to enter into
life maimed or lame, rather than
having both hands and both feet to
9 be cast into the eternal fire. And
if thine eye offend thee, pluck it out,
and cast it from thee : for it is better
for thee to enter into life with one
eye, rather than having both eyes
to be cast into the fire of Gehinnom.
10 See that ye despise not one of these
little ones ; for I say unto you, That
their angels in heaven do continually
see the face of my Father which is
11 in heaven. For the Son of Man [is
12 come] to save that which is lost. How
seemeth it to you ? if a man have an
hundred [sheep], and one of them be
lost, doth not a man leave the ninety

¹ רכב החמר.

and nine sheep in the wilderness,[1]
and goeth to seek that which was
lost ?

13   And if so be that he find it, verily
I say unto you, That he rejoiceth over
it, more than the ninety and nine

14 others which went not astray. Even
so it is not the will of your Father
which is in heaven, that one of these

15 little ones should be lost. And if thy
brother sin against thee, go and re-
prove him between thee and him
alone : and if he will hear thee, thou

16 hast won thy brother. But if he will
not hear thee, take unto thyself one
witness or two,[2] that at the mouth of
two or three witnesses every word

17 may be established.[3] And if he will
not hear them, speak unto him in
the assembly : [4] but if he neglect to
hear in the assembly, let him be unto
thee as a Gentile or a transgressor.

18 Verily I say unto you, Whatsoever ye
shall bind on earth shall be bound

---

[1] במדבר. ‏ (Cf. Luke 15 : 14.)

[2] עד אחד או שנים.

The Greek here reads עוד (more) instead of עד (a witness).

[3] כדי שעל פי שנים או שלשה עדים יקום כל דבר.
(Deut. 19 : 15.)

[4] בקהל אמור לו.

in heaven also : and whatsoever ye
shall loose on earth shall be loosed
19 in heaven also.   Again I say unto
you, If two of you shall agree on
earth [1] as touching any thing that they
shall ask, it shall be [done] for them
of my Father which is in heaven.
20 For, In every place where two or three
shall assemble in my name, there am
I in the midst of them. [2]
21   Then Kepha called [3] unto him, and
saith, Lord, how many times shall
my brother sin against me, and I
22 forgive him ? till seven times ? And
Jesus saith unto him, I say not
unto thee, Until seven times : but,
Until seventy times seven.
23   And therefore the kingdom of
Heaven is likened unto a man that is a
king, who wished to make a reckoning [4]
24 with his servants.   And when he had
begun to make the reckoning, one

¹ יבואו אחת על הארץ.

² בכל מקום ששם יקהלו שנים או שלשה בשמי שם אני בתוכם.
(Cf. Ex. 20 : 24.)
This clause is probably a quotation. Mal. 1 : 11 was also
used by the early Church in this connection.   Compare the
Didaché 14 : 1–3.

³ קרא   (we should probably read קרב with the Greek).

⁴ לעשות חשבון.

was brought unto him, which was due
to render him ten thousand minas.[1]
25 And as he had not wherewith to pay,
his lord commanded that he be sold,
and his wife, and children, and all
that he had, until full payment
should be made of what was due to
26 him. Then that servant fell down
and entreated him, saying, Give
me time,[2] and I will pay thee all.
27 And the lord had pity on his servant, and let him go, and forgave him
his debt.

28   But this servant went forth, and
found one of those who were servants
like himself, and this one was due to
render him an hundred meahs : [3] and
he seized him, and held him fast,
saying, Pay what thou art due to
29 render me. Then that servant fell
down, and entreated him, saying,
Give me time, and I will pay thee all.
30 But he would not : and went and cast
him into prison, till he should pay
31 all his debt. So when the other servants saw what was done, they were

A mina was a sixtieth part of a talent. ‏רבוא מנים.‏[1]

‏המתין לי.‏[2]

A meah was a small copper coin. ‏מאה מעות.‏[3]

exceedingly grieved, and came and related to their lord all that had happened.

32   Then his lord called unto him, and saith unto him, Servant of Belial, I forgave thee all the debt, because
33 thou didst entreat me ; and shouldest not thou also have had pity on thy fellowservant, even as I had pity on
34 thee ?   And his lord's anger was kindled, and he delivered him to the prison,[1] till he should pay all his debt.
35 So likewise shall my Father which is in heaven do unto you, if ye from your hearts forgive not every man his brother their trespasses.

19 1   And it came to pass, that after Jesus had finished speaking these sayings, he departed from Galilee, and came into the borders of Judah beyond
2 Jordan.   And great crowds followed
3 him ; and he healed them there.   And the Pharisees approached him, and tempted him, saying, Is it right for a man to put away his wife for
4 every cause ?   And he answered and saith unto them, Have ye not read, that he which made man at the

‫¹ וימסר אתו בבית האסורים.‬

beginning, made them male and
5 female,[1] and saith, Therefore shall a
man leave his father and his mother,
and shall cleave to his wife : and they
6 shall become one flesh ? [2]   And now
they are no more twain, but one flesh
only.   What therefore God hath joined
together, man cannot put asunder.[3]
7 But they said, And why did Moses
then command to give a bill of divorcement, and to put her away if she
were not pleasing in his sight ? [4]
8 And he answered them and saith,
Because Moses on account of the hard-
ness of your hearts allowed you to
put away your wives : but from the
9 beginning it was not so.   And I say
unto you, That every man that hath
put away, or shall put away [5] his
wife, except it be for fornication, and
taketh another, committeth adultery :

---

[1] זכר ונקבה עשה אותם.   (Gen. 1 : 27.)
In Matt. עשה is substituted for ברא.

[2] על כן יעזוב איש את אביו ואת אמו ודבק באשתו והיו לבשר
אחד.   (Gen. 2 : 24.)

[3] לכן את מה שחבר האלהים האדם לא יוכל להפריד.

[4] אם לא ישרה בעיניו.   (אם לא תמצא חן בעיניו.)   (Cf. Deut. 24 : 1,
The additional phrase in the Heb. Matt. lends point to the
" for every cause " of verse 3.

[5] ששלח או שישלח.

and whoso taketh the divorced [woman] also committeth adultery.

10 And his disciples say unto him, If the case of the man be so with his wife,

11 it is not good to marry. But he said unto them, All cannot accept this saying, but they to whom it is given.

12 For there are eunuchs, which were so born from their mother's womb : and there are eunuchs which were made of man : and there are eunuchs, which are self-made eunuchs for the kingdom of Heaven's sake. Whoso can accept

13 [this], let him accept [it]. Then were brought unto him children, that he should lay hands on them, and pray :

14 but his disciples rebuked them. And Jesus said, Allow the children, and hinder them not from coming unto me : for of such is the kingdom of

15 Heaven. And when he had laid hands

16 on them, he departed thence. And, behold, one drew nigh, and saith unto him, Good rabbi, and what good thing shall I do that I may acquire the life of the world to come ? [1]

17 And he saith unto him, Why askest thou me concerning what is good ?

¹ רבי טוב ומה טובה אעשה כדי שאקנה חיי העולם הבא.

There is none good but one : there
is a good, and that is God.[1] But if
thou desirest to enter into the life of
the world to come, keep the com-
18 mandments of God. And he saith
unto him, And which ? And Jesus
answered and saith, Thou shalt not
murder, Thou shalt not commit
adultery, Thou shalt not steal, Thou
shalt not bear false witness against
19 thy neighbour. Honour thy father
and thy mother : and, Thou shalt
20 love thy neighbour as thyself. But
the young man saith unto him, All
these things have I kept from my
21 youth : and what lack I yet ? And
Jesus saith unto him, If thou wilt be
perfect, go and sell all that thou hast,
and give to the poor, and thou shalt
have store in heaven ; and come and
22 follow me. But when the young man
heard the saying, he went away
troubled : [2] for he had great posses-
23 sions. Then said Jesus unto his
disciples, Verily I say unto you, That
the rich shall with difficulty enter into
24 the kingdom of Heaven. And again

---

[1] אין טוב אלא אחד יש טוב והוא האל.
[2] וילך בעצבון.

I say unto you, It is easier to pass the
camel through the eye of the needle,[1]
than to bring the rich into the king-
25 dom of Heaven.   And when the disciples heard these sayings, they marvelled exceedingly, saying, Who then
26 can be saved ?   And Jesus regarded
them,[2] and saith, On men's part this
is impossible ; but to God all such
things are possible.[3]

27   Then answered Kepha and saith
unto him, Here are we ; we have left
everything, and followed thee ; and
28 what shall we have ?   And Jesus
saith unto them, Verily I say unto
you, That ye which have followed me,
in the second birth [4] when the Son
of Man sitteth on his glorious throne,
ye also shall sit on twelve thrones,
and judge the twelve tribes of Israel.
29 And whosoever leaveth house, or
brethren, or sisters, or father, or
mother, or wife, or children, or lands,
on account of my name, shall receive
an hundredfold, and shall inherit the

---

[1] קל הוא לעבור הגמל בעד חור המחט.
[2] ויבט אליהם ישו.
[3] אצל האנשים אי אפשר זאת אבל לאלהים כל הם אפשרים.
[4] בתולדה השנית.

30 sublime life.[1] But many of the first shall be last; and the last shall be first.

20 1 The kingdom of Heaven is likened unto a man that is an householder, which went forth early in the morning to hire labourers to tend his vineyard.

2 And when he had contracted with them [2] at the rate of a zuz [3] for the whole day, he sent them into his

3 vineyard. And he went out at the third hour, and saw others standing

4 idle in the market-place, and saith unto them; Go ye also into my vineyard, and whatsoever is right I will give you. And they went their way.

5 Again he went out at the sixth hour

6 and the ninth, and did likewise. And at the eleventh hour he went out, and found others standing, and saith unto them, Why stand ye here all the day

7 idle ? And they said unto him, No man hath hired us. And he saith unto them, Go ye also into my vineyard.

8 And when it was evening, the lord of the vineyard said unto his over-

[1] החיים הנצחיים (or " perpetual life ").

[2] והתנה עמם.

[3] זוז (Gr. Ζεύς, a penny).

seer,[1] Call the labourers, and give
them their wage, beginning from the
9 first unto the last. And when those
came which came at the eleventh
hour, they received each man a zuz.

10 And when the first came, they
thought that they should have received more than these ; and they
likewise received each man a zuz.

11 And when they had received it, they
murmured against the householder,

12 saying, These last have laboured but
one hour, and thou hast put them on a
level with us,[2] which have borne the
burden of the day and the heat.

13 But he answered one of them, and
saith, Brother, I do thee no injury.[3]
Didst thou not contract with me

14 for a zuz? Take what is thine, and
go thy way : and as to my will to
give unto this last, the same as unto

15 thee, Have I no right to do what I
will in mine own sight ? Or, is thine
eye evil, because I am good ? So the

16 last shall be first, and the first last :
for many were called, but few were

17 chosen. And as Jesus went up to

[1] למפרנסו.
[2] והשוה אותם לנו.
[3] אחי איני עושה לך חמס.

Jerusalem, he took his twelve disciples privately, and saith unto them,

18 Behold, we are going up to Jerusalem ;
and the Son of Man shall be delivered
up to the chief priests and the scribes,
and they shall condemn him to death,

19 and shall deliver him over to the
Gentiles to be mocked, and scourged,
and crucified ; and the third day he

20 shall rise again.   Then drew nigh
unto him the mother of Zabdi's
children, with her sons, and did him

21 homage, and would ask of him.   And
he said unto her, What wilt thou ?
And she saith unto him, Grant that
these my two sons may sit, the one
on thy right hand, and the other on

22 thy left, in thy kingdom.   But Jesus
answered and saith, Ye know not
what ye ask.   Can ye drink the cup
that I shall drink of, and be immersed
in the immersion that I shall be
immersed in ? [1]   They said unto him,
We can.

23   Then he said unto them, Ye shall
drink indeed of my cup, and shall be
immersed in the immersion that I
shall be immersed in : but to sit on

[1] Cf. Ps. 42 : 7.

my right hand, or on my left, is not
mine to give you, but for whom it is
24 prepared of my Father. And when
the ten heard, they were displeased
25 with the two brethren. But Jesus
called them unto himself, saying, Ye
know that the chiefs of the Gentiles
rule over them, and the great ones
26 exercise authority [1] among them.   It
shall not be so among you : but whosoever among you wisheth to be great,
27 let him be your minister ; and he
among you that wisheth to be first,
28 let him be your servant : even as the
Son of Man came not to be ministered
unto, but to minister, and to give his
29 soul a ransom [2] for many. And as
they went forth from Jericho, a great
30 crowd followed him. And, behold,
two blind men went out and sat [3] by
the way side, and when they heard
that Jesus passed by, they cried out,
saying, Lord, take pity on us, O Son
31 of David. And the crowd rebuked
them, and told them to keep silence :
but they cried out the more, saying,
Lord, take pity on us, O Son of David.
32   And Jesus stopped, and called to

³ יצאו וישבו.   ² פדיון.   ¹ ישלטו.

them, saying, What will ye that I do
33 for you ?   And they say unto him,
Lord, that our eyes may be restored to
34 sight.[1]   And Jesus had pity on them,
and touched their eyes : and immediately they saw, and followed him.

21 1   And when they drew nigh unto
Jerusalem, and were come unto Beth-
phage, unto the mount of Olives, then
2 sent Jesus two disciples, and saith
unto them, Go unto the enclosure [2]
which is before you, and straightway
ye shall find there an ass [3] tied, and a
foal by her side : loose [them] and
3 bring [them] unto me.   And if any
man say aught unto you, ye shall say
that, The lord hath need of them ;
and immediately he will let them go.
4 And this was to establish what was
spoken by the prophet, who said,
5 Tell ye the daughter of Zion, Behold,
thy king cometh unto thee, poor, and
riding upon an ass, even upon a foal

---

[1] שתפקחנה עינינו.

[2] הטירה
A fenced-in area, probably constructed by pilgrims coming up
to the feast.

[3] אתון   (a she-ass).   (Also 3a and 3b, p. 141.)
It was the foal on which Christ sat, in obedience to the terms
of the prophecy.   See verse 5.

6 the offspring of an ass[3a].[1] And the
disciples went, and did as Jesus
7 commanded them, and brought the
ass,[3b] and the foal, and they put upon
them their garments, and mounted
8 him thereon. And a great crowd
spread their garments in the way ;
and others cut down leafy branches
of trees,[2] and carpeted the way.[3]
9 And the multitude that went before
him, and behind him, cried, saying,
Hoshanna to the Son of David :
Blessed is he that cometh in the name
of the Lord ; Hoshanna in the
10 heights.[4] And when he was come
into Jerusalem, the whole city was
11 seething,[5] saying, Who is this ? And
the people said, It is Jesus the
prophet, from Nazareth of Galilee.
12 And Jesus entered into the Temple of
God, and cast outside all the vendors
and buyers in the Temple, and over-
turned the tables of the money-
changers, and the stalls of them that
13 sold the doves, and saith unto them,

---

[1] אמרו לבת ציון הנה מלכך יבוא לך עני ורוכב על חמור ועל עיר
בן אתונות. ‎(Zech. 9 : 9.)

[3] ויציעו בדרך.   [2] ענפי עצום.

[5] רעשה כל העיר.   [4] הושענה בעליונות.

It is written, For my house shall be called a house of prayer ; [1] but ye have
14 made it a robbers' [2] den.   And the blind and the lame drew nigh unto him in the Temple, and he healed them.
15 And when the chief priests and the scribes saw the wonders that he did, and the children crying in the Temple, and saying, Hoshanna to the Son of
16 David ;   they were displeased, and said unto him, Hearest thou what these say ?   And Jesus said unto them, Have ye not read that, Out of the mouths of babes and sucklings
17 thou hast founded strength ? [3]   And he left them, and went without the city unto Beth - aniah ;   and lodged
18 there.   And as he returned in the morning unto the city, he hungered.
19 And when he saw a fig tree by the way side, he came to it, and found nothing thereon, but leaves only.

And he saith unto it, Let there not come forth of thee fruit for ever. And immediately the fig tree withered
20 away.   And when the disciples saw,

---

[1] כי ביתי בית תפילה יקרא.   (Isa. 56 : 7.)
[2] לסטסין.   (Gr. λῃστής.)
[3] מפי עוללים ויונקים יסדת עוז.   (Ps. 8 : 2.)

they marvelled, saying, How did it
21 immediately wither away ? And
Jesus answered and saith unto them,
Verily I say unto you, If ye shall have
faith, and doubt not, ye shall not do
such things to a fig tree only, but if
ye shall say unto this mountain, Be
thou lifted up, and cast into the sea ;
22 it shall come to pass. And whatsoever ye shall ask in prayer and faith,
23 ye shall receive. And when he was
come into the Temple, the chief
priests and elders of the people approached him as he was teaching,
saying, By what means [1] doest thou
these things ? and who gave thee this
24 means ? And Jesus answered and
saith unto them, I also will ask you
one thing, which if ye tell me, I in
like wise will tell you by what means
25 I do what I am doing.[2] The immersion of Jochanan, whence was it ?
of Heaven, or of men ? And they
reasoned with themselves, and said,
If we shall say, Of Heaven ; he will
say unto us, Wherefore did ye not
believe him ?
26   But if we shall say, Of men ; we

² עשיתי מה שעשיתי.   ¹ יכולת.

fear the crowd ; for Jochanan was in
27 the eyes of all as a prophet. And they
answered and say unto Jesus, We
know not. And he also saith unto
them, And neither tell I you by what
28 means I do these things. But how
seemeth it to you ? There was a
certain man which had two sons ;
and he approached the first, and saith,
My son, go work to-day in my vine-
29 yard. But he answered and saith, I
will not do so : but after that he
30 repented, and went. And he approached the second, and saith likewise. And he answered and saith,
I will go, lord ; but he went not.
31 Which of these two did the father's
will ? They answered him, The first.
And Jesus saith unto them, Verily I
say unto you, That the transgressors
and harlots go before you in the
32 kingdom of God.[1] For Jochanan
came unto you in the way of righteousness, and ye believed him not : but
the transgressors and harlots believed
him : and ye, when ye had seen, repented not after that, to believe him.
33 Hear ye another parable : There was

‎1 במלכות האלהים.

a man that was an householder, which
planted a vineyard, and surrounded it
with a hedge, and digged a winepress
in it, and built a tower, and delivered
it to vinedressers to cultivate it,[1] and
34 went abroad. And when the time
of the fruit drew near, he sent his
servants to the vinedressers, to receive
35 the fruits. But the vinedressers
seized his servants, and beat one,
and slew another, and another they
stoned.

36   Again he sent other servants more
than the first : and they did unto
37 them likewise. But at last he sent
unto them his son, saying, Perhaps [2]
38 they will reverence my son. But the
vinedressers, when they saw the son,
said among themselves, This is the
heir ; come, let us slay him, and his
39 inheritance will be ours.[3] And they
seized him, and brought him outside the vineyard, and slew him.
40 Think for yourselves,[4] when the lord
of the vineyard is come, what will he
41 do to these vinedressers ?   And they

(Cf. Mark 12 : 7.)

¹ לכורמים לפועלו.
² אולי.
³ ולנו יהיה ירושתו.
⁴ חשבו בלבבכם.

10

answer him and say, He will destroy the wicked vinedressers in their wickedness, and will hire out his vineyard to another, which shall render him the fruit in its seasons.

42 And Jesus saith unto them, Have ye not read in the Psalms,[1] The stone which the builders rejected is become the head of the corner. This is from the Lord, it is wonderful in our

43 eyes ? [2] And therefore I say unto you, The kingdom of God shall be taken away from you, and given to the Gentiles, which shall bring forth

44 the fruits thereof. And whoso falleth on this stone shall be broken : but on whomsoever it falleth, it will break

45 him. And when the chief priests and Pharisees heard his parables, they knew that he spake concerning them.

46 But when they sought to seize him, they feared the crowds, for he was in their eyes a prophet.

22 1 And Jesus answered and spake unto them again in parables, saying,

2 The kingdom of Heaven is likened

---

1 בתחלים.

2 אבן מאסו הבונים היתה לראש פנה מאת י׳ היתה זאת היא
נפלאת בעינינו. (Ps. 118 : 22, 23.)

unto a man that is a king, which made
3 a marriage for his son, and sent his
servants to call them that were invited
to the marriage : but they would not
come.

4   Again, he sent other servants, saying, Tell ye them which are invited,
Behold, I have prepared my banquet :
my oxen and my geese are cooked,[1]
and all things are ready : come ye
5 to the marriage.   But these remained
unresponsive,[2] and went their ways,
one to his village, another to his
6 merchandise : and the rest seized his
servants, whom with violence they
7 slew.   But when the king heard, his
anger was kindled : and he sent his
hosts, and destroyed those murderers,
8 and burned their city with fire.   Then
saith he to his servants, The marriage
indeed is ready, but they which were
9 invited were not worthy.   Go ye
therefore to the outgoing of the ways,
and whomsoever ye shall find, call to
10 the marriage.   So his servants went
forth by the ways, and gathered
together all whom they found, both
bad and good : and the marriage was

² ואלה התרשלו.   ¹ שורי וברבורי נטבחו.

filled with them that sat at table.[1]

11 And when the king came in to see them that were seated, he saw there a man not clothed with the marriage

12 garment : and saith unto him, Friend, how camest thou in hither not having a marriage garment ? And he was silent.

13   Then said the king to his servants, Bind him hand and foot, and cast him into the darkness outside ; there, shall be weeping and gnashing of teeth.

14 For many were called, but few were

15 chosen.   Then went the Pharisees, and took counsel together concerning

16 this saying.   And they sent unto him their disciples with the servants of Herod, saying, Rabbi, we know that thou art a sincere man,[2] and teachest the way of God in truth, and art not influenced by any man : [3] for thou regardest not the face of man.

17 Tell us therefore, How seemeth it to thee ?   Is it right to give tribute to

18 Cæsar, or not ?   But Jesus knew the evil in their hearts, and saith unto them, Ye hypocrites, wherefore tempt

---

[1] היושבים במסיבה   (lit. " the seated encouched ").

[2] איש אמונים.

[3] ואין עליך צניין כל אדם.

19 ye me ? Shew me a coin of the
   tribute. And they brought unto him
20 a zuz. And he saith unto them,
   Whose is this likeness and this in-
21 scription ? And they answer him
   and say, Cæsar's. Then saith he unto
   them, Give therefore to Cæsar what
   is Cæsar's ; and to God the things
22 that are God's. And when they heard
   it, they marvelled, and left him, and
23 withdrew. The same day the Zadducees, which are those that say that
   there shall not be a resurrection,
   drew near unto him, and asked him,
24 saying, Rabbi, Moses said, If a man
   die, and have no son, his brother shall
   take unto him to wife, the wife of the
   dead, that he may raise up seed to
25 his brother.[1] Now he left his wife
26 to his brother : [2] likewise the second,
27 and the third, until the seventh. And
28 after that the woman died also. In
   the resurrection whose shall she be ?
   because all the seven were her hus-
29 bands.[3] And Jesus answered and
   saith unto them, Ye do err, not know-

[1] Cf. Deut. 25 : 5, 6.
[2] There is a possible lacuna at the beginning of this verse.
[3] יען כי כל השבעה היו בעליה.

ing the Scriptures, nor the power of
30 God. For in the resurrection they
marry not, neither are they betrothed,
but are as the angels of God in heaven.
31 And concerning the resurrection of
the dead, have ye not read what was
spoken by God, who said unto you,
32 I am the God of Abraham, I am the
God of Isaac, I am the God of Jacob ? [1]
and he is not the God of the dead,
33 but the God of the living. And when
the crowds heard, they marvelled
34 concerning his teaching. But when
the Pharisees heard that he had
silenced the Zadducees, they took
35 counsel together. And one of them,
which was a doctor of the Law, asked
him, and tempted him, and saith
36 unto him, Rabbi, which is the greatest
37 commandment in the Law ? And
Jesus answered him, and saith, Thou
shalt love the Lord thy God with all
thy heart, and with all thy soul, and
38 with all thy might.[2] This is the
greatest commandment in the whole

[1] אני אלהי אברהם אני אלהי יצחק אני אלהי יעקב.
(Cf. Ex. 3 : 6.)

[2] תאהב את י׳, אלהיך בכל לבבך ובכל נפשך ובכל מאדך.
(Deut. 6 : 5.)

39 Law.[1]   And this is the first, but the
second is like unto it, And thou shalt
40 love thy neighbour as thyself.[2]   On
these two commandments hang all
41 the Law and the Prophets.   Now
while the Pharisees were assembled,
42 Jesus asked them, saying, How
seemeth it to you concerning the
Messiah ? whose son is he ?   And they
say unto him, He is the Son of David.
43 But he said unto them, And how then
doth David by his holy spirit call
44 him lord, saying, The Lord affirmed
unto my lord, Sit thou on my right
hand, till I make thine enemies the
45 footstool of thy feet ? [3]   If David
then call him lord, how is he his son ?
46 And they could not return him a
word, neither did any man wish again
to question him further from that day.
23 1   Then spake Jesus to the crowds,
2 and to his disciples, saying, On Moses'
3 seat sit the scribes and Pharisees : all
therefore that they say unto you,
observe and do ; but do not ye

---

¹ זו היא המצוה הגדולה שבכל התורה.
² ואהבת לרעך כמוך.   (Lev. 19 : 18.)
³ נאם י״י לאדני שב לימיני עד אשית אויביך הדום רגליך.
(Ps. 110 : 1.)

according to their works : for they
4 say, but do not. For they bind up
heavy and unportable burdens,[1] and
put them on men's shoulders ; but
they will not stagger about with
5 them themselves.[2] And so all their
works they do that they may be seen
of the children of men : for they
make broad their frontlets, and en-
large the corners of their mantles,[3]
6 and love the principal couches at the
7 suppers,[4] and the principal seats in
the synagogues, and benedictions [5] in
the market, and to be called of men,
8 rabbi. But ye shall not be called
rabbi : for one is your rabbi, and
that is the Messiah ; and all of you
9 are brethren. Also be not ye called
father upon the earth : for one is
your Father, which is in heaven.
10 Neither be ye called teachers : for
one is your teacher, and that is
11 the Messiah. Whoso will be greatest
among you let him be your minister.

---

[1] והם יקשרו משאות כבדות ובלתי מתנשאות.
[2] ובעצמן לא יניעו אותן.
[3] כי ירחיבו את טוטפותיהם ויגדילו כנפות כסויותיהם.
[4] ויאהבו ראשונות מושבות במשתי הערב.
[5] פרסות.

12   For whoso exalteth himself shall be
abased ;   and whoso is abased shall
13 be exalted.   Woe unto you, scribes
and   Pharisees,   hypocrites !   which
close the kingdom of Heaven against
the children of men : for ye enter not
yourselves, neither do ye allow them
14 that are eager to enter.[1]   Woe unto
you,   scribes   and   Pharisees,   hypocrites ! which devour widows' houses,
in order to pray lengthy prayers :
and therefore shall receive a lengthy
15 judgment.[2]   Woe unto you, scribes
and Pharisees, hypocrites ! which com-
pass sea and land in order to make one
proselyte, and when he is made, ye
make him twofold more a son of
16 Gehinnom than yourselves.   Woe unto
you, blind guides, which say, Whosoever sweareth by the Temple, it is
nothing ;   but   he   that   sweareth   by
the gold of the Temple, is condemned !
17 Fools and blind : whether is greater,
the gold, or the Temple that sanctifieth
18 the gold ?   And, Whosoever sweareth
by the altar, it is nothing ;   but he
that sweareth by the gift that is upon

ולא תניחו את חרוצים לבא. [1]

כדי להתפלל תפילות ארוכות ועל כן תקחו את משפט ארוך. [2]

19 it, is condemned. O blind : whether is greater, the gift, or the altar that
20 sanctifieth the gift ? He that sweareth by the altar, sweareth by it, and by
21 all things thereon. And he that sweareth by the Temple, sweareth by it, and by that which abideth therein.
22 And he that hath sworn by heaven, sweareth by the throne of God, and by him that sitteth thereon.

23 Woe unto you, scribes and Pharisees, hypocrites ! which tithe mint, and rue,[1] and cummin, and have neglected those things which are weightiest in the Law, judgment, loving-kindness and truth.

Those things ought ye to have done,
24 neither to have rejected these. Blind guides, which strain out the gnat, and
25 swallow the camel. Woe unto you, scribes and Pharisees, hypocrites ! which cleanse the outside of the cup and the dish, but within they are full
26 of extortion and uncleanness. Blind Pharisee, cleanse first that which is within the cup and dish, that the
27 outside may be clean also. Woe unto you, scribes and Pharisees, hypo-

---

[1] ‎ופינם‎ ($\pi\dot{\eta}\gamma\alpha\nu\text{o}\nu$).

crites ! for ye are like unto whited sepulchres, which appear outwardly fair to the children of men, but within are full of the bones of the dead, and
28 all uncleanness. And so ye also seem outwardly righteous to the children of men, but within you ye are full of
29 depravity [1] and violence. Woe unto you, scribes and Pharisees, hypocrites ! which build the sepulchres of the prophets, and adorn the sepulchres of
30 the righteous, and say, If we had been in the days of our fathers, we would not have been their accomplices in
31 the blood of the prophets. Wherefore ye be witnesses unto yourselves, that ye are come of them which slew the prophets, and their children ye are.
32 Fill ye up then the measure of your
33 fathers. Serpents, and generations of vipers, how shall ye escape the judgment of Gehinnom ?

34   Therefore I say unto you, Behold, I send unto you the prophets, and the wise men, and the scribes : and some of them ye shall slay and crucify ; and some of them shall ye scourge with whips in your synagogues, and

[1] נזלה.

35 persecute from city to city : that
upon you may come all the righteous
blood which hath been shed upon
the earth, from Abel the righteous
unto Zechariah the son of Berechiah,
whom ye slew between the Temple
and the altar.[1]

36   Verily I say unto you, That all
these things shall come upon this
generation.

37   Jerusalem, Jerusalem, which slayest
the prophets, and stonest them which
are sent unto thee, how many times
would I have gathered thy children
together, even as a hen gathereth her
chickens under her wings, and thou
38 wouldst not ! Behold, your house is
39 left unto you desolate. And I say
unto you, That ye shall not see me
henceforth, till ye say, Blessed is he
that cometh in the name of the Lord.[2]

24 1   And Jesus went out ; and as he
was departing from the Temple his

---

[1] Verses 34, 35 are a quotation by Christ from a Jewish
apocryphon, probably of Zechariah. The Talmud has a long
extract dealing with the murder of Zechariah. Among other
things it is said that " they killed a priest, a prophet, and a
judge, and shed the blood of an innocent man," and concerning
the deed, Ezek. 24 : 7, 8 is quoted. Cf. also 2 Chron. 36 : 14–16.

[2] ברוך אשר בא בשם יי׳.   (Ps. 118 : 26.)

disciples drew nigh in order to shew
him the buildings of the Temple.

2 But he answered them, saying, Regard
ye all these things ? Verily I say
unto you, There shall not be left here
stone upon stone, that shall not be

3 overthrown. And as he sat upon the
mount of Olives, his disciples approached him privately, saying, Tell
us, when shall these things be ? and
what sign shall there be at thy coming,
and the end of the world ?

4 Then Jesus answered and saith unto
them, Let there be no man deceive

5 you. For many shall come in my
name, saying, I am Messiah ; and
shall deceive many.

6 For ye shall hear of wars and
rumours of wars : see that ye be not
dismayed : it needs must be that such
things be done, but the end is not yet.

7 For nation shall rise against nation,
and kingdom against kingdom : and
there shall be pestilence, and famine,

8 and earthquake, in every place. And
these are but the beginning of the

9 plagues.[1] Then shall they give you over
to the tribulation, and shall slay you :

---

[1] המכאובים.

and all nations shall hate you on account
10 of my name.   And then shall many
be offended, and a man shall betray his
neighbour, yea, a man shall hate his
11 brother.   And many false prophets
shall arise, and shall lead many astray.
12   And because apostasy shall abound,
the love of many shall wax cold.
13 But whoso endureth unto the end,
14 the same shall be saved.   And this
tidings of the kingdom shall be
preached throughout the world for
a witness unto all the Gentiles ; and
15 then shall the end come.   When ye
therefore shall see the abomination
of desolation, spoken of by Daniel the
prophet, he who said that it should
stand in the holy place, (whoso readeth,
16 let him understand :) then let them
which be in Judah flee unto the
17 mountains : and he that is upon the
roof, let him not descend to take ought
18 out of his house : and he that is in the
field, let him not return to take his
19 clothes.   But woe unto them that are
with child, and to them that are about
to bear,[1] and to them that give suck
20 in those days ! And pray ye that

¹ וליולדות.

your flight be not in the winter, neither
21 on the Sabbath : for then shall be
great tribulation, such as there has
never been from the beginning of
the world until now, neither shall be
22 after it. And if those days had not
been shortened, there should no flesh
be saved : only on account of the elect
23 those days shall be shortened. Then
if any man saith unto you, Behold,
here is the Messiah, or there ; believe
24 it not. Because there shall arise false
Messiahs, and false prophets, and
shall give great signs and wonders ;
that so they may bring about, if that
were possible, the going astray of the
25 very elect. Behold, I have told you.
26 Wherefore if they shall say unto
you, Behold, he is in the wilderness ;
go not forth : behold, he is in the
27 apartments ; believe it not. For as
the lightning goeth forth from the
east, and appeareth [1] even unto the
west ; so shall be the coming of the
28 Son of Man. Wheresoever the car-
case is, there will the eagles be gathered
29 together. And immediately after the
tribulation of those days shall the

[1] ונראה.

sun be darkened, and the moon shall
not give her light, and the stars shall
fall from heaven, and the powers of
30 heaven shall be shaken : and then
shall appear the sign of the Son of
Man in heaven : and then shall all the
tribes of the earth mourn, when they
shall see the Son of Man coming in
the clouds of heaven with great power
31 and glory. And he shall send his
angels with a trumpet, and a great
voice, that they may gather together
his elect from the four winds, from the
heights of heaven to the extremities
32 thereof.[1] Learn ye the parable from
the fig tree ; When its branch is
tender, and the leaves sprout, ye know
33 that the ripe fruit [2] is nigh : so likewise
ye, when ye shall see all these things,
know that it is near, even at the doors.
34 Verily I say unto you, This generation
shall not pass away, till the whole
35 be accomplished. Heaven and earth
shall pass away, but my words shall
36 not pass away. Until that day, and
concerning that hour [3] there shall be

---

[1] ממרומי השמים עד קצוחם.
[2] Ripe fruit, especially figs ; cf. Amos 8 : 1. (read הקיץ) הקץ
[3] עד היום ההוא ועל השעה ההיא.

no man that knoweth, not even the angels in heaven, but my Father only.

37 And as it was in the days of Noah, so shall it be at the coming of the Son of

38 Man. For as they were in the days that were before the flood eating and drinking, marrying and giving in marriage, until the day that Noah

39 entered into the ark, and knew not until the flood came, and took them all away ; so shall be the coming of the Son of Man.

40   Then shall two be in the field ; one shall be taken, and one shall be left.

41 Two [women] shall be grinding at the mill ; one shall be taken, and one shall be left.

41A   Two shall be in one bed ; one shall be taken, and one shall be left.[1]

42 Be ye alert therefore : for ye know not at what hour your Lord cometh.

43 But know this, if the householder had known at what hour the thief would come, in truth,[2] he would have been alert, and not allowed his house to be

44 broken into. Therefore be ye also ready : for ye know not at what hour

45 the Son of Man cometh. Who then

[1] Luke 17 : 34.   .באמת [2]

11

is a faithful and prudent servant, whom the lord hath set over his household, that he may give them

46 bread in due season ? Happy is that servant, whom at his lord's coming unto his house he shall find so doing.

47 Verily I say unto you, That, in truth, he shall set him over all his substance.

48 But if such a servant shall say evilly in his heart, that his lord delayeth to

49 come ; and beginneth to smite the servants which are with him, and eateth and drinketh with the drunken ;

50 the lord of that servant shall come on a day when he expecteth not, and in an hour when he knoweth not, and shall surprise him suddenly,[1]

51 and appoint his portion with the hypocrites : there, shall be weeping and gnashing of teeth.

25 1 Then shall the kingdom of Heaven be likened unto ten maidens, which took their torches,[2] and went forth to

2 meet the bridegroom. Five of them were foolish, and five of them were

3 prudent. The five foolish, when they

[1] ויבקע (lit. break forth, cleave asunder). The Greek translator has failed to grasp the sense in which the Hebrew word is here used.

[2] לְפִידֵיהֶן (an oil cresset set on a long pole).

took the torches, took no oil with
4 them : but the prudent took the oil
in their vessels with the torches.
5 And while the bridegroom was de-
layed, they all slumbered and slept.
6 And at midnight there was a cry,
Behold, the bridegroom is come ; go
7 out now to meet him. Then all those
maidens arose, and made ready their
8 torches. And the foolish said unto
the prudent, Give us now of your oil ;
for our torches are extinguished.
9 But the prudent answered and said
unto them, We may not give you,
lest there suffice not for us and you :
but go now therefore unto them that
10 sell, and buy for yourselves. And
while they went to buy, the bridegroom came ; and they that were
ready went in with him to the
marriage : and the door was shut.
11 And after that came the rest of the
maidens, saying, Lord, lord, open
12 to us. But he answered, saying,
Verily, I say unto you, I know you
13 not. Be ye alert therefore : for ye
know not the day and the hour
wherein the Son of Man cometh.
14 For it is like the man which went

abroad, seafaring,[1] and which called
his servants, and delivered unto them
15 his substance. Unto one he gave five
talents, to another two, and to
another one ; to every man gave he
according to his power ; and straight-
16 way took his journey. Then he that
had received the five talents went and
traded with the same, and gained
17 other five. And likewise he that had
received the two, gained yet other
18 two. But he that had received the
one went and digged in the earth,
19 and hid it in the earth. And it came
to pass that after a long time that
lord returned, and made a reckoning
20 with them. So he that had received
the five talents drew nigh, and brought
yet other five talents, saying, Lord,
thou deliveredst unto me five talents :
and, behold, I have added unto them
yet five others.
21 And his lord said unto him, Aha ![2]
in that thou hast been a good servant
and faithful over the few ; come, and
I will give thee charge over the many :
go enter into the joy of thy lord.

[1] במדינת הים.

[2] האח (a cry of gladness. Cf. Isa. 44 : 16).

22   He also that had received the two
talents drew nigh and saith, Lord, thou
deliveredst unto me the two talents :
and, behold, I have gained these two
23 more.   And his lord said unto him,
Aha ! in that thou hast been a good
servant and faithful over the few ;
come now, and I will give thee charge
over the many : go enter into the
joy of thy lord.

24   He also that had received the one
talent drew nigh and saith, Lord, I
knew that thou art a hard man, and
reapest where thou hast not sown,
and gatherest where thou hast not
25 scattered : and I was afraid, and
went and hid thy talent in the earth :
behold, thou hast what is thine.

26   And his lord answered and saith
unto him, Thou evil and slothful
servant, thou knewest that I reap
where I have not sown, and gather
27 where I have not scattered : thou
oughtest to have delivered my money
to the money-changers, then, surely,
at my coming I should have received
28 mine own with increase. Take now
therefore the talent from him, and
give it unto him that hath the ten

29 talents. For unto whomsoever hath,
unto him shall be given, and he shall
have abundance : but whoso hath not,
from him even what he seemeth to
30 have shall be taken away. And the
idle servant, cast ye him into the
darkness outside, where there shall be
weeping and gnashing of teeth.
31   And when the Son of Man cometh
in his glory, and all his angels with
him, then shall he sit upon his glorious
32 throne : and he shall bring before
himself all nations : [1] and shall
separate them, these from those, as
the shepherd separateth the lambs
33 from the kids : and he shall set the
lambs on the right hand, and the kids
on the left hand.
34   And then shall the king say unto
them that be on his right hand, Come,
ye blessed of my Father, and possess
the kingdom prepared for you from
35 the beginning of the world. I was
an hungred, and ye gave me to eat :
I was thirsty, and ye gave me to
drink.
36   I was a stranger, and ye entertained
me : [2] I was naked, and ye clothed

[1] Cf. Jer. 3 : 17.   [2] Cf. Heb. 13 : 2.

me : I was sick, and ye visited me :
I was in prison, and ye came unto me.

37   Then shall the righteous answer
him, saying, Lord, when saw we thee
an hungred, and fed thee ? or thirsty,

38 and gave thee drink ? And when
saw we thee a stranger, and entertained thee ? or naked, and clothed

39 thee ? Or when saw we thee sick,
or in prison, and came unto thee ?

40 And the king shall answer and say
unto them, Verily I say unto you,
Inasmuch as ye have done it unto one
of these which are to me as younger
brethren, it is as if ye had done it
unto me.

41   And then shall the king say unto
them that be on his left hand, Withdraw from me, ye cursed. Get ye
into the eternal fire,[1] prepared for
Satan and his angels.

42   For I was an hungred, and ye gave
me not to eat : I was thirsty, and ye

43 gave me no drink : I was a stranger,
and ye entertained me not : I was
naked, and ye clothed me not : I
was sick, and in prison, and ye visited

44 me not.   Then shall they answer

 לכו אל אשו של עולם. ‪¹‬

them, saying, Lord, how saw we thee an hungred, or athirst, or a stranger, or naked, or sick, or in prison, and 45 did not minister unto thee ? Then shall he answer them, saying, Verily I say unto you, Inasmuch as ye did it not to one of these little ones, ye 46 did it not to me. And these shall go away into eternal punishment : but the righteous into eternal life.

26 1 And it came to pass, when Jesus had finished all these sayings, he said 2 unto his disciples, Ye know that after two days is the Passover, and the Son of Man shall be betrayed, and bound,[1] 3 that he may be crucified. Then were assembled the priests, and elders of the people, unto the court [2] of the chief priest, who was called Kaiaphah, 4 and consulted that they might secure Jesus by subtilty, and slay him.

5 But they said, Let us not do this on the feast day, lest there be a great 6 tumult [3] among the people. And as Jesus was in a certain Beth-aniah, in the house of Simon the leper, 7 there approached him a woman having in her hand a flask of precious oil,

[3] מהומה רבה.   [2] חצר.   [1] ויאסר.

which she poured upon his head, as he
8 was sitting. And when the disciples
saw it, they were vexed, and said,
9 To what purpose is this waste ? For
this oil could have been sold for
much wealth,[1] and given to the poor.
10 When Jesus knew, he said unto them,
Why molest ye this woman ? for
she hath wrought a good work upon
11 me. And the poor will be continually
with you ; but I shall not be continually with you.
12   For in that she hath cast away this
oil upon my body, she hath done it
13 for my burial. Verily I say unto you,
In every place where this good tidings
shall be proclaimed throughout the
world, there shall be told of all that
she hath done, for her name and her
14 memorial.[2] Then went one of his
twelve disciples, and it was he which
was called Judah Iscariot, and goeth
15 unto the chief priests, and saith unto
them, What will ye give me, and I will
deliver him unto you ? And they
allotted [3] him thirty pieces of silver.
16 Thenceforth he sought a convenient

בממון רב. ‪[1]‬   (Cf. Mark 14 : 5.)   על שמה ולזכרונה. ‪[2]‬
נקבו. ‪[3]‬ (The usual term for paying wages, Gen. 30 : 28.)

17 time to betray him. And on the day
before the Feast of Unleavened Bread
the disciples drew nigh unto Jesus,
saying, Where wilt thou eat the Pass-
18 over ? And Jesus saith, Go ye into
the city to such an one, and say unto
him, The teacher saith, My time is at
hand ; and with thee will I celebrate
19 the Passover with my disciples. And
the disciples did as Jesus commanded
them ; and prepared the Passover.
20 And when it was evening, he sat down
at the table with his twelve disciples.
21 And as they did eat, he said, Verily
I say unto you, that one of you shall
22 betray me. And their anger was
kindled exceedingly,[1] and each one
23 began, saying, Am I he, lord ? But
he answered and saith, He that
dippeth the hand with me in the dish,
the same shall betray me.
24   And surely the Son of Man goeth as
it is written of him : but woe unto that
man by whose hand the Son of Man
shall be betrayed ! it had been good
for that man if he had not been born.
25 Then Judah, which betrayed him,
answered and saith, Am I he, rabbi ?

ויחר אפם מעד. ‎1

And he saith unto him, Thou hast said.
26 And it came to pass, as they sat down
to eat, Jesus took the bread, and
blessed, and brake, and gave to his
disciples, saying, Take ye, and eat this
27 which is my body.   And afterwards
he took the cup, and blessed, and gave
to them, saying, Drink ye all of it ;
28 for this is my blood of the New
Covenant, which is shed for many to
29 atone for sinners.[1]   And I say unto
you, Henceforth I will not drink of
the fruit of the vine, until that day
when I drink it new with you in the
kingdom of my Father which is in
30 heaven.   And when they had recited
the psalm,[2] they went out into the
31 mount of Olives.   Then said Jesus
unto them, All ye shall be offended
in me this night.

It is written, Smite the shepherd,
and the flock shall be scattered.[3]
32 But after I am risen, I will go into
33 Galilee before you.   Then answered
Kepha and saith unto him, If they all
shall be offended, I will not be offended
34 in thee.   And Jesus saith unto him,

<hr />

¹ לכפור החטאים.   ² וכשאמרו את התחילה.

³ הך את הרועה ותפצנה הצאן.   (Cf. Zech. 13 : 7.)

Verily I say unto thee, That this night,
before the cock crow, three times shalt
35 thou deny me. Then Kepha saith
unto him, Even if I must die with
thee, I will not deny thee. And so
36 likewise said all the disciples. Then
cometh Jesus with them unto a
village [1] whose name was Ge-shemanim,[2] and saith unto his disciples,
Sit ye here, while I go yonder and
37 pray. And he took with him
Kepha and the two sons of Zabdi,
and began to be grieved and down-
38 cast. And then said he unto them,
My soul is grieved unto death : await
ye me here, and watch with me.
39 And he passed on a little, and fell on
his face, and prayed, saying, O Father,
if it be possible that this cup pass
away from me, let it be done : but
let it not be done as I will, but as
40 thou wilt.[3] And he cometh unto his
disciples, and findeth them sleeping,
and saith unto Kepha, Could ye not
41 watch with me a single hour ? Watch

---

[1] לכפר.

[2] ני־שמנים. (The fertile valley, Isa. 28 : 1.)

[3] אבי אם אפשר שיעבור הכוס הזה ממני עשה אבל לא יהי
כרצוני אלה כרצונך עשה.

and pray, that ye enter not [into temptation] : [1] the spirit indeed is
42 watchful,[2] but the flesh is frail.   He went away again the second time, and prayed, saying, O Father, if this cup cannot pass away from me, but I needs must drink it, be it as thou
43 wilt.[3]   And he cometh again, and findeth them sleeping : for their eyes
44 were heavy.   And he went away again, and prayed the third time, and said the same prayer as he had said
45 already.   Then cometh he unto his disciples, and saith unto them, Ye have slept now, and taken your rest : behold, the hour is at hand wherein the Son of Man shall be given into
46 the hands of sinners.   Arise, and let us go : behold, he draweth nigh that
47 betrayeth me.   While he was yet speaking, behold, Judah, one of his twelve disciples, came, and with him a great force with swords and spears,[4] that were sent from the chief priests
48 and elders of the people.   Now Judah,

---

[1] Carelessly omitted.   שוקדת. [2]

[3] אבי אם לא יוכל לעבור הכוס הזה ממני אלא צריך שאשתה
אותו יהי כרצונך.

ורמחים. [4]

who betrayed him, had given a sign
to those people which came with him,
saying, Whomsoever I shall kiss, that
49 same is he : secure ye him. And
forthwith he approached Jesus, and
saith, Peace, rabbi ; and kissed him.
50 And Jesus saith unto him, Beloved,[1]
wherefore art thou come ? Then they
drew near, and laid hands on Jesus,
51 and seized him. And, behold, one of
them which were with Jesus put forth
his hand, and drew his sword, and
struck the servant of the chief priest,
52 and cut off his ear. Then said Jesus
unto him, Return thy sword unto its
place : for all they that take the
sword shall perish with the sword.
53 Thinkest thou that I cannot ask of
my Father that he should send now
on my behalf more than twelve
54 legions [2] of angels ? But how then
shall the Scriptures be established,
which have written that thus it must
55 be done ? In that same hour said
Jesus to the crowds, Are ye come out
to meet me as against a robber [3] with
swords and spears to secure me ?

---

[2] לִנְיוֹנִי. (Gr. λεγεών).

[1] אָהוּבִי (or friend).
[3] לִיסְטֶס (Gr. λῃστής).

Every day I sat beside you[1] and taught you in the Temple, and ye
56 seized me not.   But all this has come to pass to establish the Scriptures of the Prophets.   Then all the disciples
57 forsook him and fled.   So they seized Jesus, and led him unto Kaiaphah the chief priest, where the scribes and the elders were gathered together.

58 And Kepha followed him afar off unto the court of the chief priest, and entered into the house,[2] and sat with the menials, to see what would be the end.

59 Now the chief priests, and the whole council, sought false witness against Jesus, to deliver him up to death.

60 But they found none :   though there came forward many false witnesses.   But at the last there came
61 two false witnesses, and said, He said, I can pull down the Temple of God, and ere three days I can build it.

62 Then the chief priest arose, and saith unto him, Answerest thou nothing at all concerning these things which they witness against thee ?

[2] אל הבית.   [1] אצלכם.

63 But Jesus answered nothing, but was silent.

Then the chief priest said unto him, I adjure thee by the living God, that thou tell us whether thou be Messiah,
64 the Son of God.   And Jesus answered and saith unto him, Thou hast said.

Wherefore I say unto you, Henceforth ye shall see the Son of Man, that sitteth on the right hand of the power of God,[1] coming in the clouds
65 of heaven.   Then the chief priest rent his garments, saying, He hath blasphemed.

What further need have we of witnesses ?   behold, ye have heard
66 now that he hath blasphemed.   How seemeth it to you ?   And they answered, saying, He is condemned to
67 death.   Then they spat in his face, and struck him with the fist ;   and others put their hands upon his face,[2]
68 saying, Prophesy unto us, O Messiah,
69 who it is that assailed thee.   Now Kepha sat without in the court : and there approached him a maid-servant,

[1] היושב מימין כח האלהים.
[2] ואחרים שלחו את הידים אל פניו.   (Cf. Mark 14 : 65.)

saying, Thou too wast with Jesus the
Galilean.

70   But he denied in the sight of all,
saying, I know not what thou sayest.

71 And when he was going out to the
door,[1] another maid-servant saw him,
and saith unto them that were there,
He also was with Jesus the Nazarene.

72   And again he denied with an oath,

73 and said, I do not know him. And
after a while they that stood there
drew near, and said unto Kepha, In
truth thou art [one] of them ; for thy

74 tongue revealeth thee. Then began
he to curse and to swear that he knew
not that man. And immediately the

75 cock crew. And Kepha remembered
the words of Jesus, who had said,
Before the cock crow, three times shalt
thou deny me. And forthwith he
went outside, and wept bitterly.

27 1   And it came to pass in the morning,
that all the chief priests and elders
of the people were in conclave together [2] concerning Jesus in order to

2 condemn him to death. And they
bound him, and led him away, and
delivered him to Pontius Pilate the

ונוסדו יחד. ²   וכשהוא יצא לדלת. ¹

12

3 governor. Then Judah, who had betrayed him, saw that he was condemned to death, and he repented, and brought again the thirty pieces of silver which had been given him,[1] and gave them to the chief priests and
4 elders, saying, I have sinned in that I have betrayed the blood of the righteous. But they said, What is
5 that to us ? see thou to it. And he cast the thirty pieces of silver into the Temple,[2] and hanged himself with
6 a halter.[3] And the chief priests took the pieces of silver, and said, It is not right to cast them into the treasury, for they are the reward of blood.
7 And they took counsel, and bought with them the portion of the potter's field, for the burial of strangers.
8 Wherefore the portion was called
9 Chakel-damah [4] unto this day. Then was fulfilled that which was spoken by Jeremiah the prophet, who said, And they took the thirty pieces of silver, a goodly price of him that was

---

[1] אשר נתנו לו.
[2] That is, he threw them into the treasury chests.
[3] ויתחל בפח.
[4] חקל דמה.

valued, whom they valued of the
10 children of Israel ; and gave them
for the potter's portion, as the Lord
11 appointed me.[1] Now Jesus stood
before the governor : and the governor
asked him, saying, Art thou king of
the Jews ? And Jesus answered him,
12 and saith, Thou sayest. But when
the chief priests and elders slandered
him, he answered them nothing.
13 Then said Pilate unto him, Hearest
thou not the testimony which they
14 witness against thee ? But he answered him nothing, not even a single
word ; insomuch that the governor
15 marvelled exceedingly. Now on the
feast day it was customary for the
governor to bring forth to the people
16 one prisoner, whom they would. And
they had then in custody a certain
prisoner, a brigand,[2] whose name was
17 called Bar-Rabbah. Therefore when
they were assembled, Pilate said unto
them, Whom will ye that I release

---

[1] ויקהו את שלשים הכסף אדר היקר היקור אשר הוקירו מאת
בני ישראל ויתנו אותם לחלקת היוצר כאשר העיד בי י״י.
(From a lost writing of Jeremiah ? See note, Chapter II. ; cf.
Zech. 11 : 13.)

[2] פריץ.

unto you ? Bar-Rabbah, or Jesus
18 which is termed Messiah ? For he
knew that for hatred they had de-
19 livered him up. And when he was
set down on the judgment seat,[1] his
wife sent unto him, saying, Have thou
nothing to do with that righteous
man : for I have suffered many
20 things this day because of him. But
the chief priests and elders persuaded
the people to ask Bar-Rabbah, and
21 destroy Jesus. And the governor
answered and saith unto them,
Whether of the twain will ye that I
release unto you ? And they said,
22 Bar-Rabbah. And Pilate saith unto
them, What shall I do then with
Jesus which is called Messiah ? And
they all answer and say, Let him be
23 crucified. Then the governor saith
unto them, But what evil hath he
done ? And they repeated [2] and cried,
24 Let him be crucified. Then Pilate
saw that he could prevail nothing, for
a great tumult arose. Therefore he
took water, and washed his hands
before the people, saying, I am innocent of the blood of this righteous

² והם ח.   (Gr. βῆμα.)   בימה ¹

25 man : see ye to it. Then answered
all the people, and said, His blood be
26 on us, and on our children. Then
released he Bar-Rabbah unto them,
but delivered Jesus unto them to be
scourged with whips, and crucified.[1]
27   And then the soldiers [2] of the
governor took Jesus, and delivered
him unto them in the court of justice,[3]
and gathered unto him the whole
28 crowd. And they stripped him, and
29 robed him in a scarlet tunic, and
encircled his head with thorns for a
crown, and placed a reed in his right
hand, and bowed their knees before
him, and mocked him, saying, Peace
30 be with thee, king of the Jews ! And
they spit upon him, and they took
the reed, and smote him on the head.
31 And after that they had derided him,
they stripped him of the tunic, and
clothed him in his own garments, and
32 led him away to be crucified. And
as they were going out, they found
a man of Cyrene, whose name was
Simon ; and him they brought to.

---

[1] ואת ישו מסר להם ליסרו בשוטים ולהצלב.

[2] סטרטיוטין. (Gr. στρατιῶται.)

[3] ומסר להם בבית דין.

33 carry his cross. And when they
were come unto the place which is
34 termed Golgoltha,[1] they gave him
wine mingled with opium : [2] and
when he had tasted, he would not
drink.

35 And after they had crucified him,
they parted his garments, and cast
lots : to fulfil that which was spoken
by the mouth of the prophet, who
said, They part my garments among
them, and upon my vesture they
36 cast lots.[3] And they sat down and
37 guarded him. And they set his sentence above his head, and thus it was
written, This is Jesus king of the
38 Jews. Then were crucified with him
two robbers, one on the right hand,
39 and one on the left hand. And all
they that passed by were reviling
40 him, and nodding their heads, saying, Aha ! thou that destroyest the
Temple of God, and in three days
buildest it, save thyself. If thou be
the Son of God, come down from the
41 cross. And likewise the chief priests
reviled him, with the scribes and

[2] בראש.   [1] גלגלתא.

[3] יחלקו בגדי להם ועל לבושי יפילו גורל.   (Ps. 22 : 18.)

42 elders, saying, He saved others ; but himself he cannot save. If he be the king of Israel, let him now come down from this cross, and we will
43 believe in him. He trusted in God ; let him deliver him now, if he delight [in him] : for he said, I am the Son
44 of God. And so likewise the robbers, which were crucified with him, re-
45 proached him. Now from the sixth hour there was darkness over all the
46 land until the ninth hour. And at the ninth hour Jesus cried with a loud voice, and saith, My God, my God,
47 why hast thou forgotten me ?[1] And some of the men that stood by, when they heard, said, He calleth for
48 Elijah. And one of them ran straightway, and took the sponge,[2] and filled it with vinegar, and put it on a reed,
49 and gave him to drink. But the others said, Let be, and let us see if
50 Elijah will come to deliver him. Then Jesus cried again with a loud voice,
51 and yielded up his spirit. And, behold, the veil of the Temple was rent in twain from the top to the bottom ;

[1] אלי אלי למה שבחתני. (Cf. Ps. 42 : 9.)

[2] הספוג. (Gr. σπόγγος.)

and the earth did quake, and the
52 rocks were rent ; and the sepulchres
were opened ; and many bodies of
the saints, which were laid [to rest],
53 arose, and went forth from the
sepulchres after his resurrection, and
entered into the holy city, and were
54 seen of many. And the centurions [1]
which were with Jesus, to guard him,
when they saw the earthquake, and
those things that were come to pass,
were exceedingly afraid, and said, In
55 truth, he was the Son of God. Now
many women were there beholding
afar off, which followed Jesus from
56 Galilee, ministering unto him : among
whom were Miriam the Magdalene,
and Miriam [the daughter of] Jacob,
and the mother of Joseph, and the
57 mother of Zabdi. And when it was
evening, there came a certain rich
man from Ramathaim,[2] whose name
was Joseph, and he also was a disciple
58 of Jesus. And he approached Pilate,
and asked the body of Jesus. Then
Pilate commanded the body of Jesus
59 to be given. And Joseph took the
body of Jesus, and wrapped it in

² הרמתים.   ¹ ושרי המאה.

60 pure linen,[1] and placed it in his new
sepulchre, which was hewn out of
the rock. Then he rolled the great
stone over the door of the sepulchre,
61 and went his way. And there were
there, Miriam the Magdalene, and the
other Miriams,[2] sitting over against
62 the sepulchre. Now on the next day,
which was [the day] following the
inquisition for leaven,[3] the chief priests
and Pharisees came together unto
63 Pilate, saying, Lord, we remember
that this deceiver said, that, Ere three
days after my death [4] I will rise again.
64 Therefore give command to guard the
sepulchre until the third day, lest his
disciples enter, and steal him away,
and say unto the people, that he is
risen from the dead : so the last error
shall be worse than the first.

65   And Pilate saith unto them, Behold, ye have a guard ; go, and keep
66 guard as ye know [best].   So they

---

[1] בסדין. (Gr. σινδών.)

[2] ואחרות מרים. (Cf. John 19 : 25.)

[3] בדיקת חמץ.

(In agreement with John, and Jewish tradition that Jesus was
crucified on the eve of the Sabbath (Friday), and the day
before the Feast of Unleavened Bread.)

[4] אחרי מותי.

went, and made the sepulchre in-
accessible with guards,[1] and sealed
the stone.

28 1 Now on the evening of the Sabbath,
as it dawned toward the first day of
the week,[2] came Miriam the Magdalene
and the other Miriam to see the
2 sepulchre. And, behold, there had
been a great earthquake : for the
angel of the Lord had descended from
heaven, and approached and rolled
away the stone from the door, and
3 sat upon it. And his appearance was
like lightning, and his garments like
4 snow : and for fear of him the guards
5 trembled, and became as dead. And
the angel answered and said unto the
women, Fear ye not : I know that ye
6 are seeking Jesus. He is not here :
for he is risen, as he said. Come now,
and see the place wherein the lord
7 was laid. And go now straightway,
and tell his disciples that he is risen
from the dead ; and, behold, he goeth
before you into Galilee, and there shall
ye see him : and, behold, I have told
8 you. And they went forth quickly
from the sepulchre with fear and great

---

² באחד השבת.   ¹ ויבצרו הקבר בשומרים.

joy ; and ran to tell his disciples.
9 And as they were going to tell his
disciples, behold, Jesus came to meet
them, saying, Peace be with you.
And, behold, they approached and
held him by the feet, and did him
10 homage. Then said Jesus unto them,
Fear ye not : go now and tell my
brethren that they go into Galilee,
11 for there shall they see me. And
when they were gone away, behold,
some of the guards came into the
city, and told the chief priests all
that had come to pass. And when
12 they had assembled the elders, and
had taken counsel, they gave much
13 money to the soldiers, saying, Say ye,
That his disciples came by night, and
stole him away while we lay down.
14 And if this should be heard by the
governor, we will persuade him, and
15 secure you. So they took the money,
and did as they were taught : and the
saying is common among the Jews
16 until this day. Then his eleven disciples went away into Galilee, unto a
mountain where Jesus had appointed
17 them. And they saw him, and did
him homage : but some doubted.

18 And Jesus approached and spake unto them, saying, All authority is given 19 me in heaven and earth. Go ye therefore, and teach all the Gentiles, and immerse them in the name of the Father, and the Son, and the Holy 20 Spirit : and teach them to observe all that I have commanded you : and, here am I with you all the days, unto the end of the world.

APPENDIX A

HEBREW AND ARAMAIC GOSPELS AMONG THE JEWS TO A.D. 600

T. B. Shabb, 116, *a, b.* "Imma Shalom was the wife of R. Eliezer and sister of Rabban Gamliel. There was in her neighbourhood a 'philosoph,' who had got a name for not taking a bribe. They sought to make fun of him. She sent to him a lamp of gold. They came before him. She said to him, I desire that they divide to me the property of the women's house. He said to them, Divide it. They said to him, For us, it is written, Where there is a son, a daughter does not inherit. He said to them, From the day when ye were exiled from your land, the Law of Moses has been taken away, and the law of the Evangelion עון גליון has been given, and in it is written, ברא וברתא כחדא ירתון, A son and a daughter shall inherit alike. The next day he (R. Gamliel) in his turn sent to him a Lybian ass. He said to them, I have looked further to the end of the book, and in it is written, אנא לא למיפחת מן אורייתא דמשה אתיתי ולא לאוספי על אורייתא דמשה אתיתי I am not come to take away from the Law of Moses, and I am not come to add to the Law of Moses, and in it (the Law of Moses) is written, Where there is a son, a daughter does not inherit."

The whole of this passage is in Aramaic, so that the Gospel citations prove nothing as to language. Nevertheless, it is probable that a Hebrew or Aramaic Gospel is referred to. The second quotation is distinctly Matthæan. The date may be about A.D. 80.

189

Justin Martyr (*Dial. with Trypho the Jew*, ch. x.) : "*Trypho* : Moreover, I am aware that your precepts in the so-called Evangelion are so wonderful and so great that I suspect no one can keep them ; for I have carefully read them."

Here again the language is uncertain. Trypho appears to refer to the Sermon on the Mount in Matthew's Gospel The date is about A.D. 140.

T. B. Shabb, 116a. " R. Meir called it Aven-Giljon, און גליון ; R. Jochanan called it Avon-Giljon, עון גליון."

These plays on the word Evangelion (Gospel) were made in the second and third centuries respectively.

Origen (*Against Celsus*, Bk. II. ch. xiii.) : " This Jew of Celsus continues, after the above, in the following fashion : Although he could state many things regarding the events of the life of Jesus which are true, and not like those which are recorded by the disciples, he willingly omits them."

Celsus seems to refer to an early form of counter-Gospel in use among the Jews. See below, under *Toldoth Jeshu*.

Epiphanius (*Against Heresies*, xxx. 3.) : " Others again have asserted that the Gospel of John is kept in a Hebrew translation in the treasuries of the Jews— namely, at Tiberias—and that it is hidden there as some converts from Judaism have told us accurately."
 Ibid. (xxx. 6.) : " And not this alone, but also the Gospel of Matthew, which was originally Hebrew."

These extracts from Epiphanius are on the authority of Count Joseph, a Judæo-Christian and physician to Hillel, the Jewish Patriarch of Tiberias, in whose possession the Gospels were, and who is said to have made a death-bed confession of his faith in Christ.

Finally, we must refer to a form of counter-Gospel in various rescensions which took definite shape in the fourth and fifth centuries, and was commonly known among the Jews as the תולדות ישו (*Toldoth Jeshu*)

"The Generations of Jesus." The contents of this document show distinct acquaintance with the canonical Gospels as well as some apocryphal traditions, while the title points directly to Matthew, it being customary among the Jews to name their books after the opening words. The oldest forms of the *Toldoth* are found in both Hebrew and Aramaic.

BIBLIOGRAPHY

Christianity in Talmud and Midrash. R. Travers Herford, B.A.

Works of Justin Martyr. Ante-Nicene Christian Library.

Works of Origen. Ante-Nicene Christian Library.

Paralipomena. Bernhard Pick, Ph.D., D.D.

Das Leben Jesu nach Jüdischen Quellen. Samuel Krauss.

APPENDIX B

HEBREW AND ARAMAIC GOSPELS IN THE POS-SESSION OF JEWISH AND OTHER CHRISTIANS TO A.D. 600

Papias quoted by Eusebius (*Eccl. Hist.*, Bk. III. ch. xxxix.):
"Matthew composed the oracles in the Hebrew dialect, and each translated them as he was able."

Irenæus (*Against Heresies*, Bk. III. ch. i.):
"Matthew also issued a written Gospel among the Hebrews in their own dialect, while Peter and Paul were preaching at Rome, and laying the foundations of the church."

Origen quoted by Eusebius (*Eccl. Hist.*, Bk. VI. ch. xxv.):
"The first (Gospel) is written according to Matthew, the same that was once a publican, but afterwards an apostle of Jesus Christ, who having published it for the Jewish converts, wrote it in the Hebrew."

Eusebius (*Eccl. Hist.*, Bk. III. ch. xxiv.):
"Matthew also, having first proclaimed the Gospel in Hebrew, when on the point of going also to other nations, committed it to writing in his native tongue, and thus supplied the want of his presence to them by his writings."

Epiphanius (*Against Heresies*, xxx. 3):
"And these too (the Ebionites) receive the Gospel according to Matthew; for this they too . . . use to the exclusion of the rest. And they call it ' according to the Hebrews,' to tell the truth because Matthew alone in the New Testament set both the

exposition and preaching of the Gospel in Hebrew speech and Hebrew characters."

Jerome, *Catal. Script. Eccl.* :

"Matthew, who is also Levi, and who from a publican came to be an Apostle, first of all the Evangelists composed a Gospel of Christ in Judæa in the Hebrew language and characters, for the benefit of those of the circumcision who had believed : who translated it into Greek is not sufficiently ascertained. Furthermore, the Hebrew itself is preserved to this day in the library at Cæsarea which the martyr Pamphilus so diligently collected. I also was allowed by the Nazarenes who use this volume in the Syrian city of Berœa to copy it. In which it is to be remarked that, wherever the Evangelist . . . makes use of the testimonies of the old Scripture, he does not follow the authority of the Seventy translators, but that of the Hebrew."

Isho'dad, *Comment. on the Gospels* (trans. by Mrs. Gibson, p. 9) :

"His (Matthew's) book was in existence in Cæsarea of Palestine, and every one acknowledges that he wrote it with his hands in Hebrew," etc.

The following early writers either possessed or had access to Hebrew or Aramaic Gospels : Papias, Hegesippus, Justin Martyr, Tatian, Symmachus, Irenæus, Pantænus, Clement of Alexandria, Origen, Pamphilus, Eusebius, Epiphanius, and Jerome.

Eusebius (*Eccl. Hist.*, Bk. V. ch. x.) :

"Pantænus . . . penetrated as far as India, where it is reported that he found the Gospel according to Matthew, which had been delivered before his arrival to some who had the knowledge of Christ, to whom Bartholomew, one of the Apostles, as it is said, had preached, and left them that writing of Matthew in Hebrew letters."

13

Jerome (*De Vir.*, iii. 36) completes the story :

"Pantænus found that Bartholomew, one of the twelve Apostles, had there preached the advent of our Lord Jesus Christ according to the Gospel of Matthew, which was written in Hebrew letters, and which, on returning to Alexandria, he brought with him."

Several of the Apocryphal Gospels bear superscriptions stating that they were written in Hebrew, with the obvious intention of commending them as genuine Apostolic productions. This claim may perhaps be supported in the case of the *Book of James* and the *Acts of Pilate*. The superscription to the *Gospel of pseudo-Matthew*, which is closely allied to the *Book of James*, may serve as an illustration :

"Here beginneth the book of the Birth of the Blessed Mary and the Infancy of the Saviour. Written in Hebrew by the Blessed Evangelist Matthew, and translated into Latin by the Blessed Presbyter Jerome."

In referring to Apocryphal Gospels we exempt the *Gospel of the Hebrews*, so widely used by the Judæo-Christian communities, which has every right to be considered as a canonical Gospel, if it be not the parent of them all. That it was so considered for several centuries the Fathers themselves are witnesses ; and that it ceased to be so is due to gradual corruption, and to the unique situation in which its audience was placed as a distinct body of Jewish believers. At least two rescensions of this Gospel are known to us, both probably in Aramaic, and we may classify them as Epiphanian and Hieronomian after the two writers who have chiefly preserved their contents. Jerome, it is true, translated the whole Gospel into Greek and Latin, but no copies are known to have survived. The famous Cæsarean MS. may have been the very one brought back by Pantænus from India, having descended through Clement of Alexandria to Origen, who may have brought it to

APPENDIX B 195

Cæsarea, where, with the rest of Origen's collection of MSS. it may finally have passed into the hands of Pamphilus who deposited it in his library. The library is believed to have been burnt by the Arabs at the capture of Cæsarea in A.D. 653. The last we hear of a Hebrew Gospel is in the ninth century. Cod. Tisch. 3 (Λ), a Greek MS. of the Gospels, dating from this period, having in Matthew four marginal quotations from "the Jewish," one of which is identical with one of Jerome's quotations from the *Gospel of the Hebrews*.

BIBLIOGRAPHY

The Gospel according to the Hebrews. E. B. Nicholson, M.A.
The Author of *Supernatural Religion.*
Eusebius' *Ecclesiastical History.* C. F. Crusé, A.M.
The Ante-Nicene Christian Library.
Isho'dad Commentaries on the Gospels. M. G. Gibson, D.Litt., LL.D.

PRINTED BY
MORRISON AND GIBB LIMITED
EDINBURGH